Those Not-So-Still Small Voices

God Says the Most Amazing Things Through Your Kids

Thom Hunter

NAVPRESS

BRINGING TRUTH TO LIFE
NavPress Publishing Group
P.O. Box 35001, Colorado Springs, Colorado 80935

The Navigators is an international Christian organization. Jesus Christ gave His followers the Great Commission to go and make disciples (Matthew 28:19). The aim of The Navigators is to help fulfill that commission by multiplying laborers for Christ in every nation.

NavPress is the publishing ministry of The Navigators. NavPress publications are tools to help Christians grow. Although publications alone cannot make disciples or change lives, they can help believers learn biblical discipleship, and apply what they learn to their lives and ministries.

Cover illustration: Frances Middendorf

Printed in the United States of America

FOR A FREE CATALOG OF
NAVPRESS BOOKS & BIBLE STUDIES,
CALL 1-800-366-7788 (USA)
or 1-416-499-4615 (CANADA)

Contents

Can two walk together, except they be agreed?
Amos 3:3, KJV

*This book is dedicated to you, Lisa, my wife,
with whom I walk. I love you.*

*And this book is dedicated to our children,
because their love made it possible.
Thank you Zachary, Russell, Donovan,
Patrick, and Lauren.*

Introduction

Listening to the Not-So-Still Small Voices

So use every piece of God's armor to resist the enemy. . . . In every battle you will need faith as your shield . . . the helmet of salvation and the sword of the Spirit—which is the Word of God.
Ephesians 6:13,16-17, TLB

W hen I was seven, I lived with my family in an old frame house on Texas Street, right next to the Santa Fe Railroad tracks and only two blocks from a creek crawling with crawdads. Our house was a house of character, surrounded by huge cedar trees and overgrown rose bushes. We had a wraparound porch . . . the perfect stage on which to play out any small boy's dreams.

This dream house had a huge attic . . . the dark and mysterious kind . . . a part of the house I never entered, never explored. There was an opening into this attic through the ceiling over the hallway leading to the kitchen. While I had never found the courage to go there, in my daydreams I battled many an attic foe with my daddy at my side. Daddy never feared the attic or anything beyond. If Daddy was in his easy chair or sitting at the kitchen table, I could walk beneath that attic opening with not so much as a shudder, with not so much as a thought of the darkness beyond the opening.

One day, though, my mother sent me down that long,

shadowy hallway to the kitchen to fill a pitcher full of water for dinner. I couldn't, wouldn't go. Not beneath the attic opening. Daddy had gone away and suddenly it really was a threatening, brooding attic . . . not a doorway to a magical cave filled with buried treasure or great adventure. My daydreams were shattered in the face of a nightmare.

Reality is frightening when faced alone. I was only seven, but I had unwillingly discovered there was a whole lot of reality out there in the world, coming after me. And though my mother would spend her whole life rising to the occasion of being a single parent, the absence of my father shaped me.

When I was twelve, I had a great friend named Will. Will had the perfect family, and therefore, all my envy. To me, any family with a mom and a dad was pretty nearly perfect. But I realized, as I came to know Will better, that the attics he encountered while alone, he entered with as much fright as I did mine. Any reality that tracked him down found him standing meekly on his own.

A curious thing, I thought. There's more to having a daddy than just having one.

It is funny—well, no, it isn't funny—how mine and Will's generation learned to embrace new family structures, to respond cooperatively to psychologists and counselors telling us to free ourselves from "binding, loveless marriages." Fathers have become, to many, a discretionary commodity—nice to have around but not exactly essential. A bonus, if you will.

So now we have a new generation of fathers, men who contribute the spark to begin a new life, but aren't exactly sure of their role in fanning the flame of this new life. So now we have a new generation of children being raised by fathers of uncertainty.

I once was a fearful child, choosing paths of caution to avoid attics of uncertainty, wondering who would answer my cries in the darkness, fearing I had done something wrong, worrying I wasn't learning something Daddy should be there to teach me.

And then I was a father, with a son of my own expecting me to do the natural daddy thing, whatever that was.

Curious thing, I thought. There's more to being a daddy than just being one.

When my oldest son, now fifteen, was seven, we stood in our yard on a crisp, winter Sunday afternoon, sharing a football and the snowfall.

"I can kick it higher than you," he said. "Farther than you. Straighter than you. I bet I can kick it better than anybody in the whole wide world."

And he tried. And he missed. And I threw him the ball and he dropped it. And he missed some more. And he kicked it once or twice, a couple of yards. And once he kicked it and it flipped over his head and landed behind him.

"Watch," I said, laughing at him. And I kicked the ball over our house. Our two-story house.

When I turned for applause, I found tears.

Zachary stood with his hands in his jacket pockets. I suddenly felt very tall and very large and very powerful. His shoulders slumped and his head dropped between them until his teary eyes focused on his wet right tennis shoe, the one that had failed to kick the ball.

And then he went into the warm house and left me shivering in the yard, the sight of his tears biting into me with more ferocity than the winter winds. My own warm tears thawed my cheeks.

Zachary didn't know what his silent retreat taught me that morning. But much more clearly than ever before, I realized I have a privileged, planned place in my children's lives. That we are together is not an accident, a happenstance of nature. It is a carefully planned, God-approved arrangement. Not something to be taken lightly.

"How special he is to God," I thought. "And how special I must be to God to be trusted with him, and all my children."

Under the frigid sky, I confessed my fear and uncertainty. The door to a long-feared attic of my own began to open as I looked inside myself.

"Don't let me mess it up," I said simply to God. "I'm afraid I'm not ready. I don't know if I know what to do."

There was no sound except my own breathing and the cold breezes rattling the stiff, empty branches of the trees. I stood alone, and listened.

And then I went back into the house to find my son. I was convinced that that was what God wanted me to do. That was the answer. Find him. Talk to him. And listen.

Just listen. Listen to the not-so-still small voices, my valuable children, individually molded with the Creator's unmatchable skill, singled out for His purpose but so easily sidelined by my own indifference.

God—the Father—would tell me what to do. He would not abandon me in my uncertainty. He would find no pleasure in my stumbling in the dark.

Where once I was alone, He now walks with me down the hallway beneath the attic door and calms my fears. And together we fill the pitcher.

I do not know how any parent can succeed without God's lead.

1
Pondering the Pandemonium

I came through the door, draped my coat in its regular place on the arm of the rocking chair, and crossed the living room. No one heard me, and for a few seconds I stood silently in the doorway, like a shopper outside a window display longing for something in the window, something too valuable, too precious, too costly. Maybe even beyond my worth.

I viewed the scene with all those feelings, but with an underlying assurance as well. The precious items were already mine. My family.

At this moody moment when afternoon burns itself out and dusk descends, no one was missing. Our dining room, though lacking the technology of a traffic-control tower, rivals the city airport for takeoffs and landings. Everybody reports in—the hungry, the hurt, the angry, the dirty, the conquered, and the conquering. Here they beat their chests or bind their wounds. Our dining room is the ultimate in a multi-use facility.

In it are devoured three meals a day, uncountable

snacks of questionable nutrition, gallons of milk, and ever-flowing water to quench never-ending thirsts. While the table is the centerpiece, cars race across the floors, banging against chair legs and human shins. Wooden blocks knock cars off the train track. The tile floor is mottled by the remains of modeling clay and splats of watercolors. Puzzle pieces lie here and there.

The dining room telephone is the busiest. Everything from "I missed the bus. Can you come get me?" to long, drawn-out discussions of the value of baseball cards.

The kitchen counters are comfortable for leaning against during deep conversations, lighthearted visits, or after-school confessions. The light in the kitchen-dining room springs on in the morning and fizzles out at midnight with a sigh.

And so I stand unnoticed, the worn table in focus. The fruit of knowledge—homework—is being served, and the appetites are despairingly weak.

Lisa stands with her back to the kids. She is chopping onions to add to a pan of frying potatoes. The smell makes me glad I am home in time to enjoy not only the meal, but the smells of preparation.

How, with four disgruntled children at the table, in various phases of muttering or shouting protests against doing homework while the sun still shines, can she hold the knife steady and still hum? Is it a defense mechanism, or does she just thrive on chaos?

Lauren, a four-year-old beauty, her hair pulled loose from her ponytail, a chocolate-chip cookie smudged on her chin, has her place at the head of the table. She alone does not protest. She thumbs quietly through a stack of books, making her own humming noises, kicking her feet against the broken highchair that should have been put into the attic years ago. She's no baby anymore.

Patrick, seven years of freckles and usually all smiles, looks hurt, bent over, with his elbows obscuring most of the worksheet he is working on. The deep, dark pencil scribbles across the top of his paper mean something is wrong. He'll tell me exactly what it is pretty soon.

Donovan is staring out the patio door. Hoping for a rescuer to take him away from all this? He's nine, and a good student, but books clash with Lego soldiers and boats and castles. If he could sneak past Lisa, he'd be up to his room and his creations.

Russell is, of course, barefoot and wearing his Tae Kwon Do outfit, or "gih," as he refers to it. With his mother turned away, he crosses his arms in the air and grimaces, knocking invisible foes to the ground, keeping the world safe for geography—the subject he is ignoring.

"Russell, sit down and get back to work," she says, dropping potatoes into the hot oil. How did she know? He was being perfectly silent.

Zachary, thirteen and back in his room, is the only one taking his work seriously. Quite seriously. He isn't happy about it, but he knows he'll never get to play basketball if he doesn't get through pre-algebra first. He has to be a mathlete before he can be an athlete. And the sun always goes down too early.

I can hear him now, "Just two more baskets?"

Where did all these people come from? There was no hint of this fifteen years ago when Lisa and I made a commitment to each other.

I never dreamed how elastic that commitment could be, how easily it could be expanded and reshaped without being weakened. It seems I came home from work one day and there were all these new, little creations crowded around a table, waiting for potatoes to fry and Daddy to walk in the door. Bless my soul.

My eyes moistened and I cleared my throat. Over all the loud protestations, my presence was immediately known and the manageable chaos over which Lisa was reigning fell apart. She was breaking open ice trays now . . . a sound that always makes me hungry.

"Daddy!" Lauren shrieked. "Look. I finished my homework before all the boys. And *they* go to school."

I held out my hand like a traffic cop as the kids crowded around. Zachary came from his room. I can't help but feel concern about the coming day when Daddy's coming home doesn't pull people to the door.

"One at a time," I said and took Lauren's drawing from her blue marker-colored hands.

"This is a picture of my family," she explained.

I looked at the three lumpy figures on the smudged sheet. One was obviously a mommy—it had hair. The other was me—it had glasses. And the other was undoubtedly Lauren—it had a bow. All had stick arms and legs and the little one in the middle was reaching up to hold hands with the bigger lumps.

"But, Lauren. Where are the boys?"

"On the back where they belong," she explained. "They're back there if we ever need 'em."

On the back of the picture, equally smudged, were four little blobs with stick arms and legs and big smiles. Nothing distinguished any of them except one had freckles. Undoubtedly Patrick.

"Why dotted lines?"

"So I can cut them apart if I need one of them and also to keep them from holding hands. Boys don't do that."

And then I was swamped with stories about their day. A teacher who had been harsh. A teacher who had been great. A bully on the playground. A lost lunch. A scraped elbow. New birds in the nest in the neighbor's tree. A completed metal-arts project. A chance to make the honor roll. A paper to do over because "the teacher said my mind was elsewhere."

And then, lo and behold, books disappear and a meal appears. All those frayed edges of protest soften and there is laughter and teasing and sharing. Not to say this always happens at the Hunter table. There are times when more than bread is broken—like hearts by cruel comments, or glasses by clumsy, racing reaches for the last piece of bread itself. But tonight, it's as if Lisa has read the mood and produced the food that fits it. This table, around which so much of our lives revolves, is good.

Two hours later, with the dishwasher grousing, the children demolishing their rooms, and Zachary and friends trying to break the record for friends on a three-way call, I came across Lauren's picture on top of the day's trash in the kitchen.

Grease and ketchup stains looked natural on the stick figures. I took the picture from the sack. My kids create thousands of them, in the car, in church, in bed probably, with the lights out. But I wanted to save this one along with others that have touched my heart with permanence.

Then I noticed that the drawing had changed. On the front, Lauren had added a big, thick, wavy arrow to the edge of the paper. On the back, she'd erased the dotted lines and redrawn all the hands. Now the boys were reaching up, holding hands.

I know, it's because when *I* came home, she realized we're all one big family. She felt bad about sticking the boys on the back, to be called forth "only if we need them." Aren't I a great dad? My very presence makes everyone see how closely we are knitted together.

"I almost let this get thrown away," I said to Lisa, who was passing by with four glasses of water in her hands, heading down the hall. "I'd never forgive myself if this had stayed in the trash."

"I'm sorry," she said, with well-earned tiredness. "I thought it was just a greasy sheet of paper someone left on the table."

"Don't you see?" I said. "Don't you see the love here?"

"I see grease and ketchup and wrinkled paper," she said. "The love is down the hall."

All Lisa could really see, she admitted, was that Lauren

had had too small a piece of paper and had put the boys on the back. Out of sight, out of mind.

"We've been running out of space ever since Donovan was born," Lisa said, continuing her trek down the hall. "Lauren isn't unaware."

I continued to search the drawing for some deeper meaning as Zachary bounded into the room, making pretend jump-shots across the living room toward the kitchen. The dishes were all done; it was time to eat again.

"Milk . . . and that's all," I said.

He guzzled a glass, watching me stare at first the front and then the back of Lauren's picture. My initial burst of self-pride was wearing off. She probably hadn't picked up so much from my presence that she would rush and revise her drawing.

"Oh cool," said Zachary. "You found our picture."

"*Our* picture?"

"Mine and Lauren's."

And then he set me straight. Between phone calls and radio-hit countdowns, he'd found time to sit unnoticed at the kitchen table with his little sister, amid all the dinner debris, and discuss family life. By the end of their conversation, the drawing—ketchup and grease and all—had new life. Deeper meaning. Significance to make it worth saving.

Had thirteen-year-old Zach really explained that everyone's in a family all the time? Not just "on call"? Apparently he didn't like the idea of being stuck on the back of the sheet, "just in case."

"We drew the arrows and erased the dotted lines," he said. "She was happy."

He rinsed his glass, a sign that Mom's persistence pays off—at least in small measure—and he headed back to his room.

"Turn your music off and read a while before lights out," I said, studying the drawing further. "Zach? Whose idea was it to redraw the arms on the boys?"

"Mine," he grinned sheepishly. "But don't tell anybody. It's just that Lauren said boys can't ever hold hands, but I told her *brothers* can . . . in pictures."

And then he entered *his* room and closed *his* door and played *his* music. I flipped the picture back and forth and thought back to the busy moment when Lauren had first showed it to me and I had simply said, "That's nice."

Zachary had seen more and said more and done more. And at least three members of this family had been touched.

I compromised with Zachary, stopping at his room on my way down the hall to turn his boom box down instead of off, giving him the benefit of the doubt that he could read his library book and absorb something other than the repetitious lyrics on the radio.

If I'd never been in this house, I could have found the rest of the boys blindfolded. They were far outdoing the boom box. The noise did more than drift down the hall, it shook the pictures, caused the carpet fibers to lean in the direction of the sound waves, and occasionally set the dog to barking in the back yard. But a person with a blindfold would have regretted it, for the hall was booby-trapped with pieces of Lego and slime had been dabbled on the doorknob.

This is "tucked in"?

They were anxious for evening prayers. I know I was, but first came the usual bed check for illegal weapons, inappropriate tools, and midnight provisions. Before we can pour forth the prayers, we have to peel back the sheets.

Russell had his practice set of rubber numchucks—a Tae Kwon Do weapon he intended to use in a most unplaylike way on a younger brother once the dark got good and settled in. I took them, despite his threatening karate-chop stance. His wiry body is all muscle, but it's still small, and though he leaps into action at the slightest provocation, he also smiles and giggles. Number two son is not a warrior yet.

Patrick had a package of post-tooth-brushing Jujyfruits poorly hidden in his pajamas. He leaned forward to get a final drink, they fell to the floor, and I snatched them up. Oh, how I love Jujyfruits. I promised to take care of them for him.

Donovan's bed was clear of contraband, except for the tooth under his pillow. A front tooth. One worthy of ceremony for all the blood it had spurted after a week of wiggling. That one tooth dominated Donovan's face. If anything could ever draw attention away from the ears God gave him, the absence of the tooth came close.

I checked my pockets for quarters. I *will* not forget. I will *not* forget.

"Pray for soldiers and missionaries and babies-to-be," said Donovan.

We always pray for soldiers, even when war is not raging, for Donovan is, at this point in his life, a soldier at heart. And we always pray for missionaries because my college room-mate is in Colombia. But this "babies-to-be" is a new request. Donovan has heard something somewhere that is troubling him. I decided to pray first and ask questions later.

The other boys poured forth with prayer requests ranging from the banishment of all bad dreams to an eternal suspension of rain. Eventually I called a halt, realizing that while their hearts are generally in the right place, they're using sudden piety to stretch bedtime.

By the time I finished praying, Donovan had started squirming.

"You were supposed to do that before you got into bed," I said. "Now hurry up."

He did hurry too, dashing down the hall like an Olympic sprinter. Then he returned, leaping from the center of the room neatly into bed and burrowing his head into the pillow, making sure the tooth was still there.

I turned out the lights and left the pungent odor of dirty socks behind as I headed down the hall. It was Friday night, but they should never have been allowed to skip baths.

A little voice intruded from Lauren's room as I walked by.

"A person could die without water," she moaned. One of Lisa's four glasses of water must have gone in Lauren's room, but probably had been shared with various wetting baby dolls, all of which were making little puddles somewhere in the dark.

By the time I got back from the kitchen, Lauren was asleep, her soft, pudgy legs dangling over the side of the bed where she had leaned back waiting for me. Her long, blonde hair draped across her eyes, and her mouth was puckered like a sweet kiss. When I moved her further up into her little bed, she made soft sounds of protest, but clutched her elephant blankie and sailed away.

Four down. One to go.

It was then I noticed it was ten o'clock and I still had my tie on. The kids were an hour late to bed and I *still* had my tie on. This was not successful parenting. But who's to know?

I could hear the washing machine going through its familiar cycle shifts. Someone's sneaker pounded against the dryer door. The garbage disposal was grinding the remains of uneaten vegetables the kids had snuck away from. Obviously, Lisa is running a little late, too.

These familiar sounds are music. The harmony of home.

At least it is quiet in the dark at the end of the hall. The bedrooms are still and silent. Or so I believed.

The crash that followed sounded fatal. Images of madmen crashing through the bedroom window flashed through my mind. Glass shattered and something fell. A chorus of terrified screams pierced the night and then there was silence. I paused at half-hall. I heard whispering and identified the voices of all three younger boys, frantic but apparently safe and well. The lights were still out.

Putting my wrath under semi-control, I headed for the door and flipped the light switch. Nothing. Still darkness.

"Turn on the closet light," I demanded.

"I might cut my feet," Russell said meekly, guilt dripping from each monosyllabic word.

After crunching my way to the closet, further reducing the floored ceiling light fixture and bulb remains beneath my shoes, I demanded an explanation. It was the familiar story of numchucks in the night.

"I barely tossed them," Russell said. "I guess I don't know my own strength."

"He was trying to kill me," said Donovan.

"And he almost killed all of us," added Patrick.

As I picked up the pieces, I assured Russell he would soon know his own strength. It would be put to the test over the next few days through a series of special chores to earn money for a new light fixture. After all, he'd have some extra time on his hands, as he'd be going nowhere. Then I turned out the closet light.

"Daddy?" came the quiet, still voice of Patrick, who had been pondering the pandemonium. "Do those prayers we said earlier still count, or is God mad, too?"

"Don't you worry, Pat. Prayers *always* count."

"Well, that's good, 'cause I thought we were going to have to do them all over, and I think I just want to get some sleep."

And then he was gone dreamin'. And everyone was asleep, so I laid the numchucks beside Russell's head, pulled the covers up around Patrick's neck, and placed the four quarters under Donnie's pillow.

"Thanks, Dad," Donovan said. "Good night."

The hamster was in his cage. The refrigerator door was closed. All was right in the world. Lisa was running her bath, seeking the warm waters of replenishment. An ambulance raced by in the distance, its lonely siren setting the dog to howling.

Missy's pitiful scratching at the patio door said "feed me, for I have been patient, but I bite the hand that feeds me if it lags too long in duty." Somehow, Zachary and Lisa had forgotten, for I am admittedly third in line when it comes to pet care.

Missy satisfied, I closed the patio door and turned out the kitchen light, which went out in a blaze of glory. Yes, I would know this room more for its memories than its menus. The refrigerator hummed on peacefully. In the attached laundry room, the tennis shoes gave up their quest for freedom as the dryer stopped. The house was closing down.

"Zachary," I said, knocking on his door on the way to my room. "Good night. Turn out your light."

The little ribbon of light around his closed door disappeared and I heard him drop his book to the floor and turn over on his side with a loud yawn.

And then it hit me. Somehow, with little protest from him, I had unconsciously stopped his bedtime prayers. Had I become wrapped up in his teenage image of self-sufficiency? Had I assumed that by closing his door, he was sending a message that I was not welcome inside? If I had thought that, I suddenly thought just as strongly that I was wrong. So I knocked again.

"Hi," I said, blinding him with the light. "Got a few minutes?"

I love Zachary's room. He says it's not cool enough, but to me his walls reflect a certainty and confidence I lacked when I was thirteen. No wonder he retreats here so often. I would too if he didn't have such a strong claim to it. The walls project his dreams: from million-dollar race cars to bungee-jumping, slam-dunking to space-walking.

We prayed about the future, everything from his aching knees to his algebra test. We prayed about a friend whose father had died, a new kid at school, for God's guidance and forgiveness, and we thanked God for His love. And I thanked God for Zach.

After we finished, I apologized to Zach for forgetting to come and pray with him.

"Mom's been taking care of it," he said.

I should have known.

As I paused at his door, I could hear the bath waters

draining from the tub. Barely above the noise, Lisa was humming.

"You know, Zach," I said. "You sure are getting tall."

"G'night, Dad," he said.

Five down.

All small voices now at rest, kissed and covered and fully blessed, I untied my tie, fully certain I am where God wants me. What a privilege to be home.

2

A Reason for Rising

S aturday bloomed nice and peaceful . . . somewhere. But not in my bedroom.

"I've got to be at Young Astronauts by eight o'clock," yelled Russell, pounding on the bathroom door. "Why does it always take you so long in there?"

"There's nobody in there," I said, pulling my head very slowly from underneath my pillow. "I'm still over here."

"You mean you're not even out of bed yet?" he cried, pouncing on me and pulling at the covers. "I knew I'd be the last one there again. I'll get ignored if I'm the last one there. I won't even get to be in on the experiments. I may as well not even go."

"Russell, it's 7:15. It takes ten minutes to drive to Young Astronauts. Go take a space walk."

Russell's intrusion was only the beginning. My feet touched the floor and I was rubbing my eyes, staring at the dark clouds and pounding rain outside my window when Zachary came in: "When can we shoot my BB gun?" followed by Donovan: "Help me build a boat," and Patrick:

"You promised to practice T-ball with me."

I emerged to the accompaniment of thunder and Lisa stood at the door, buried behind piles of dirty sheets she had already stripped from the children's beds. What is this? The whole world will stop revolving if I pause to rub my eyes?

She informed me that the pancakes were all mixed up, but Aunt Jemima'd flown the coop. Would I be a good daddy and run to the store for some syrup? I'd sooner eat them with ketchup than go out before my morning shower. However, behind all that laundry and a forced smile was a serious woman.

I just love Saturday mornings.

Lightning split the dark clouds as I pulled on my clothes and headed outside, mumbling under my breath.

"You always wake up in a bad mood, you know it," Zachary said.

"I do not," I growled back, thundering out the door and splashing off the porch. Across the soggy yard, I addressed myself therapeutically: "I am the head of the household. That's why I'm doing this. I am a provider. I care. I want breakfast."

No one's at the supermarket on Saturday mornings before eight except ugly people buying Aunt Jemima from slow checkers and sleepy bagboys. And I was the ugliest, as my reflection in the glass door showed. The thinner my hair gets, the worse it looks uncombed. Add a little rainwater and it's indescribable.

Some women still wear pink foam curlers, I noticed. And heavyset men venture out in the early morning hours, shirtless, to buy donuts. Young mothers without makeup, their hair pulled back tight, rush in with babies still in pajamas to buy milk and Froot Loops. We all stood in line, pretending not to notice how ugly we all were in our natural state, when in walked the firemen, all pressed and straight, in finest uniform, to buy orange juice and bagels for the station.

I will exercise. I will do situps. I will eat salads for lunch.

I will not eat strawberry cream-cheese croissants on the way to work again as long as I live. And I will live longer for all these promises.

All of this, I told myself, will start as soon as I finish my pancakes. I had come out at my ugliest in this awful weather, and I was going to have my pancakes—butter, syrup, and all.

Russell swallowed his pancakes whole and licked his sticky fingers in the van on the way to Young Astronauts.

"Do you really want to be an astronaut?" I asked as we sat at a red light.

"We never make this light," he answered, as tense as a bank robber with police in pursuit. "Why do we always have to stop at this light?"

"Because it's always red when we get to it," I said patiently. "Now, do you really want to be an astronaut?"

"I don't know," he said. "I want to be a Tae Kwon Do master. But Brad wants to be an astronaut."

"So, you've signed up for forty weeks of Young Astronaut training because Brad wants to be an astronaut?"

"Brad's my best friend."

"Of course," I said. "I just wish it wasn't so early on Saturdays."

"Why?" he said. "All you have to do is wake up and drive me over here. I have to do all the work. Besides, maybe I will become an astronaut. I'm only ten years old, Dad. I don't have to decide yet. Who knows, maybe Brad will become a Tae Kwon Do expert, or maybe the President will decide all future astronauts have to know Tae Kwon Do to go to Mars. Who know's what's on Mars."

The light changed.

I started through the intersection, assuming Russell was dreaming about Mars. I was. I'd always wanted to go there. In fact, I wanted to be an astronaut too, but my zeal was permanently diffused by a ninth-grade algebra teacher who told me I was mathematics-deficient and always would be. She gifted me with a D and a sigh and washed her hands of me.

"Dad!" Russell screamed.

I slammed on the brakes and looked to see if someone hadn't slid on the slippery streets into the intersection. All clear. I looked in the mirror to make sure I wasn't going to get rammed from behind. No one there. Only Young Astronauts and ugly pancake freaks are out this morning, I reminded myself, so the traffic is light.

"I forgot my notebook! I can't go without my notebook. It's got all my drawings in it. I'm the best drawer in the world. Brad will think I'm stupid. Everybody will think I'm stupid. I'm not going."

Russell's trademark Disneyesque tears . . . still there after all these years and greatly out of proportion to his eyes, were beginning to form rivers on his cheeks.

What to do. What to do. Should I make him responsible for his actions and let him suffer his shame in silence with public humiliation in front of legions of Young Astronauts? Or should I turn around and head home for the notebook? Should I berate him for his forgetfulness and lash out from my perch of perfection or allow him to pass as a typical absent-minded fourth grader whose mind is so full of imagination that reality occasionally gets crowded out?

We all forget things. Obviously, or I wouldn't have had to swim to the supermarket in dawn's early light.

I made a circle through a convenience store parking lot and we headed home, caught again by the red light.

"Uh, Dad?" Russell said sheepishly as the light changed. "I've got my notebook. I forgot I threw it in the back seat because I was in such a hurry to get in the van because of the rain. You're not mad, are you? Want to see my drawings of the space shuttle?"

I should have looked at those drawings before. Every Saturday, he faithfully tucked his notebook under his arm and headed to a two-hour class, giving up his one free morning. Many nights he labored at his desk and I had failed to ask to see his drawings.

"Yes, I want to see."

I had to turn the van around again, this time sneaking through a service station parking lot. We headed back toward the school and the light turned red again just in front of us.

While we waited, Russell showed me his drawings of the space shuttle and of a space station he'd designed, complete with a Tae Kwon Do workout chamber. His drawings were good, the work of a vivid imagination that believed in itself.

Russell has no fear of dreams and no timidity in sharing them with others. He hopped out of the van and splashed through every puddle on the path to meet his fellow dreamers.

Some of the greatest inventions of man were first scratched out roughly with a pencil by imaginative ten-year-olds who, like Russell, were certain their ideas could fly, or heal, or entertain. Someday, someway, these inventions would work.

It had taken me three stops through the red light, but I was suddenly swept with a reason for rising on Saturday mornings. There's a lot that can't be learned beneath a pillow.

The red light caught me again. I glanced in the rear-view mirror and saw Russell's notebook, lying on the seat, open to his drawings. He forgot it.

The light changed again, I went through the service station parking lot, made a U-turn, and had to wait through the light again to head back to the school with his notebook and the world's best space shuttle drawings. No doubt he'd be expecting me.

No matter what the rest of this Saturday morning would bring, be it a rainbow or an all-day deluge, I had been refreshed at the red lights, enjoying brief moments of revelation. It hadn't been a heart-to-heart talk, but a little volunteered insight. Little snapshots to be crowded into a larger book of everlasting memories. How many of those do I miss when nothing slows me down?

On the way home, I made all the lights.

I just love Saturday mornings.

3

Like My Father Before Me

"Ask your mother."

That line always worked before, buying me a little respite from the curious questions that come at me every time I am at rest. The frustrated expression on the solemn face before me made it clear my own personal wisdom was being sought. Apparently, this was not a question to be sent to the kitchen and answered amid flying potato peels. It was put down the book, set aside the soft drink, make some room on the sofa, and pay close attention time. Now, what was the question?

"Okay, Donovan," I said, unconvincingly. "I'm all ears. What's on your mind?"

"I asked," he said softly, trailing a single finger across his chin, "why don't you ever talk about your daddy? Didn't you like him?"

"And I said, 'Ask your mother'? Sorry, Donnie, I guess I was a tad self-absorbed."

I put away the book, made room on the couch, and prepared to confront myself and provide an answer to my most searching son. How could Donovan rise from behind a plastic Lego castle, having spent more than an hour in raging fantasy, and confront me with such piercing reality? It is as if he has always had a map of my inner self and when he sees things that don't look familiar, he wants to sightsee in the depths of my soul. I have found him to be a critical tourist with a sharp eye, never satisfied without the whole story. His first word, as a wide-eyed curious babe, should have been *why*.

We got comfortable. This was a question for which an answer can't be blurted. It is a question that must be answered right the first time, with honesty. What my son has really asked me is if I loved my father . . . and if I did, why are my memories of that love unknown to my own son?

"Is this a trick question?" I asked, stalling for time. "No? I didn't think so."

I remembered back, to a time when I myself was a not-so-still small voice . . . timid and soft. I was seven.

"Daddy," I said, "how do you keep the jelly from oozing out on the cookie sheet? Mommy and I tried to make these at home and they sorta blew up in the stove."

We were in the kitchen part of my daddy's one-room apartment in an old brown building in downtown Fort Worth. Mike, my brother, and Deb and Sue, my sisters, were on the balcony watching the red neon bank sign revolve on top of the building across the dark alley. But me? I was in my version of Heaven, alone with my daddy, making jelly rolls and talking. Just my daddy and me.

"I take a little water and mash them together on the edges," he said. "Want to know a secret? If no one's watching, I use spit. It works better than anything."

Now I knew how to do it. When Mommy turns her head . . . spit on 'em.

In a few minutes, Daddy would call in his other children and we'd eat jelly rolls so hot the steam rose out of the cracks in the dough, and he'd tell stories, probably about frog gigging or boot camp. His stories were all old . . . as if life had quit happening a few years back. But they were glorious stories, and better with each visit to his dark, little flat with the gray walls and huge, screenless windows so big you could walk right out them. My daddy lived in a different world, one without clocks and dirty clothes hampers and other things that organize life into when and where.

Daddy didn't like organization. He liked crickets for pets and enjoyed racing June bugs across the hardwood floor, placing penny bets. He liked sitting up all night, watching the lights of the city flicker out, listening to the sirens, the cats, and the mosquitoes. He liked writing poetry, and when he was sober, he was good.

And I was sure he liked me. Though some doubt would creep in on weekends when he didn't call to tell us which bus to take down the interstate. But on the good weekends, he'd meet us at the station and we'd walk to the park. He was strong and the merry-go-round would fly. Once I was so dizzy when I got off that I walked right into a nearby tree and busted my nose. Fortunately, Daddy always carried a handkerchief.

He loved pinto beans with cornbread and sour pickles. And Fig Newtons. And Vienna sausages on crackers with mustard. And barbecued Spam. And Viceroy cigarettes. And frog gigging. And war stories. And me?

Donovan waited patiently as all those memories raced through my mind. It only took a couple of minutes. There are so few.

"Donovan, I will tell you two stories about my daddy," I said.

I was only six when Daddy first took me frog gigging on the pond at his sister's farm in tiny Bridgeport, Texas. She boasted she had the noisiest pond in Wise County, so brimming with frogs she could serve their fried-up legs three meals a day and still the croaking would keep you awake at night. "I live," she'd cackle, "in frog heaven."

It was midsummer and the sun set just before nine, finally dropping the temperature below 90. Daddy and I went out in the boat alone, to glide across the still, black pond to the far side where the frogs were thickest. The stars in the clear country sky were so bright and colorful they looked like glitter.

The frogs fell silent at our intrusion.

"Shhh," Daddy said, putting his fingers to his lips. "If we're real quiet, they'll forget we're here and they'll make some noise . . . then . . . scrack! . . . from the lily pad to the frying pan."

I was as quiet as I had ever been in my life, and within an hour we had ten fat frogs in two minnow buckets and we were headed for shore. I can almost hear Aunt Nell cackling now: "Better than catfish, tastier than fried chicken, and a definite fine source of protein. Yes sir, it's frogs that make your hair shine."

We'd caught them, Daddy and me. A silent hour in a boat, surrounded by mysterious darkness, rocking gently on a summer night with strange sounds surrounding us. I felt secure, loved, wanted. There was no need to talk, for words could be spread out over the years until someday, as two men, we'd trap this night's surviving frogs' great-grandsons.

The next day, in the bright and honest morning light, with countless frogs dug into the cool mud to escape the sun's merciless heat, Daddy left. He never returned. Aunt Nell fried the frog legs, but I couldn't eat. I could only cry. Tears are like tiny, tidy keys locking doors on hurts.

"That's sad," Donovan said, looking straight into my eyes. "So, I guess that's why you never talk about him."

"But he is my daddy and he is your grandfather, and I should tell you all I can about him. So, I'll tell you another story. And in a minute, I'll show you the only thing I have that belonged to my daddy."

We children had gathered once again in tiny Bridgeport, this time for our father's funeral. It was a strange feeling, for I hadn't seen him in several years. I knew I should feel sad—he was my dad—but I just didn't.

Daddy died the way he lived . . . all alone in a gray little flat in Fort Worth on a cold February night. It was an uncomfortable funeral, full of the people who would have loved him if he had only let us. No tears, just lots of furrowed brows and wondering expressions. He'd spent his life, but none of us really knew how.

Debbie and Sue cleaned out his room, throwing away piles of clutter . . . tobacco cans, pickle jars, balls of used aluminum foil, broken transistor radios, old clothes . . . the remnants of a tightly woven life.

Among the clutter, she found a box of yellowed writing tablets, pages and pages of thoughts and memories recording the years of a lonely existence. Proof that this man cared about many things, thought about nearly everything, felt sorrow and happiness, confusion and concern, anger and frustration, longing. . . .

I couldn't wait to get the tablets home and learn about my dad. For days after the funeral I studied the scratchy handwriting and began to create in my mind a more accurate picture of my father and the things that mattered to him. On these rambling pages were the war stories, told as clearly as if they had happened yesterday, and yes, glorious tales of frog gigging.

As I read further, I came across simple stories that detailed his daily life, like the ones about his crickets:

"When I lived in apartment number 40, I had two crickets in the house. I listened to them so much I could tell them apart. So I caught them, and the one with the lightest chirp, I named it Marge. I took a bottle of fingernail polish and put one red dot on its back. And I caught the other one and put two dots on its back and called it Harry. People could hardly believe me when one would tune up and I would say, 'There goes Marge,' or 'There goes Harry.' I won a lot of quarters on that one."

But more than anything, he wrote about his loneliness.

"It's Saturday night again. All I can say is that it already has the feel of sadness and it's not even sundown yet. Now it's sundown and as I watch the golden sun set, I'm more lonelier than ever. But soon it will be over and I only have to watch the darkness. And you never know what lurks in the darkness of the night.

"I've said before that no one has ever seen me cry. And I don't think anyone will ever see me cry. It's a sign of weakness. I guess I've done my share of crying, but no one ever saw me. I wonder what's gonna happen to me next?"

I closed the tablet and put my arm more tightly around my son.

"You know, Donovan, when I first read that, I cried. I was thinking back to when I was sitting on a dark, still pond in the black of a peaceful night with my daddy. He wasn't alone that night, and the dark was a beautiful thing, because we shared it. And though it was shattered by the bright morning, I never forgot that night.

"Did I love my daddy? Yes, I did. And I think I would have liked him a lot, if he had let me. You probably would have liked him too. And I know he would have liked you."

"Well, I was just wonderin'," said Donovan, packing his Legos and heading upstairs to his room. He stopped. "Can we make some jelly rolls some time?"

"You bet."

"Can I spit on 'em?"

"Only when I'm not lookin'."

Someday, I'll tell Donovan more about what I learned from my daddy's diaries. You see, after spending hours poring over the pages of his life, I was struck silent by one painful revelation. In the carefully recorded memories of his sixty-two years, my name was not to be found.

I've thought since then how important it is to make it

clear to our children how much they mean to us. To make it clear that they are more than just a small measure in our life. I know from experience that children doubt sometimes, no matter how obvious we try to make our love.

Daddy probably loved me. He may have remembered me intruding on his life, back when I was just a small voice. Maybe those memories were just too personal, or perhaps too painful to put on paper. I wonder. Unfortunately, I did that a lot growing up. Wondered, that is.

But Donovan will not have to wonder. Nor will Russell, or Patrick, or Lauren, or Zachary. I say it in the dark. I say it in the light. And here it is, on this page: "I love you."

Just ask your mother.

4

Once in a Lifetime

As a little boy growing up in various Texas towns without a father at home, my goal was always not to be just a father when I grew up, but to be a daddy. I knew I had a father somewhere, but I didn't have a daddy, and boy, was I envious.

The number one responsibility of a daddy, I told myself through the years, is to "be there," not to miss the events, momentous and miniature, that bind the father to the son. All my life, I catalogued events of my own that I would have shared with my own daddy. "Someday," I vowed, "I'll enjoy these things anew, with my own children. Someday."

Somedays *do* arrive. And they usually arrive when we are least prepared for them, bogged down in our work, overscheduled, fatigued, in demand by things to which we've committed ourselves. In the midst of making our to-do lists a small voice will zero in: "You *will* be there, won't you? Daddy?"

"Of course," I answer, clearing my throat. "Wouldn't miss it."

The year was 1984. The busiest year of my adult life. The year after the birth of what I mistakenly thought would be our last child and our fourth son. It was the year of my first first grader's first first-grade picnic. Yes, it was a momentous year.

And I almost did miss the picnic, drowning in my own deadlines, but I fled from the office just in time and sped to the school.

Zachary sat hunched over near the picnic table, twisting blades of grass, the sun beating down on his brown neck poking out of his T-shirt. His hair was turning lighter and his skin darker. He was dirty from the playground, scraped on both elbows, sweaty, and his socks hung limply over the tops of his once-white tennis shoes. He sat alone, surrounded by a thousand—or at least seventy-five—seven-year-olds.

His eyes were following something intently as it journeyed through the tall grass, and when the fleeing creature would almost get beyond his reach, he would throw out a finger roadblock. He was busy with his actions but absorbed in his thoughts.

"Oh good," he said as I sat down on the grass beside him. "I was afraid you wouldn't get here before the gold bug got away. Look."

I saw then that it really was a goldish, shiny bug fleeing from Zachary in the grass. I thought about what he'd said: "before" the gold bug got away. He had never imagined that I might not show up at all, that I might have forgotten the end-of-the-first-grade Washington School picnic. It was a once-only moment in his life.

Surrounded by a hundred or more moms, Zachary and I ate our sandwiches in the sun together, sitting on the grass, my legs cramping, my knee joints stiffening. He pointed out various kids and told me their names. Every now and then a child would drift by and ask Zach, in hushed tones, "Is that your dad?"

Every time they asked, I wanted to lose forty pounds on

the spot, change into a sporty tennis outfit, and flex my muscles to give Zach something to be proud of. But Zach looked right at me, just as I was, and beamed when he answered, "Yes, he sure is."

We didn't really do much at the picnic. Zach wanted to make sure his teacher knew I came. He wanted to walk around a little and show me the sights of the park. He introduced me to Rachel, whom he chases and who chases him. He pointed out the boy who read the most books, the kid who broke his arm and never cried. He shared his Chiclets with me and had a hard time believing I chewed Chiclets way back when I was seven.

"Did you share them with your dad?" he asked.

That evening, after we both got home, we watched thunderclouds come closer and closer, as we sat in lawn chairs on freshly mowed grass, pulling ticks off the dog. In every cloud he saw a tornado, wanting the tornado to come just close enough so we could see it up close, but not close enough to blow anything away . . . except maybe that old barn where the snakes live.

When the rain started to fall, we retreated to the front porch and watched it pour, and I told him how my grandmother had a porch so long you could run a relay on it. On ours, you stood shoulder-to-shoulder.

In the top corner of the porch, though, there was a birds' nest the boys had been dying to see inside of. Zachary had earlier dragged a chair out onto the porch and stood on his tiptoes—still several inches short. Struggling to lift him high enough to see inside, I was amazed at how heavy a seven-year-old is.

He peeked inside. No eggs yet, but some grass and feathers waiting.

"Did your dad ever lift you up to see inside of a bird's nest?" he asked.

At the end of the evening, in his room, decorated with the heroes and the dreams of his young life, I tucked him in for the night. He showed me the certificate he got for reading 100 books, so I asked him to read me a bedtime story, and he did.

He showed me the cage he had built for the frog he'd catch in the morning. He asked me to help him catch it and I said I would.

Zachary lay on his stomach and I rubbed his back until his eyes closed. Only when I got to the door did I find he was just pretending, as he shouted out, "Good night . . . Daddy!"

And then I went downstairs alone to ponder bedtime stories, seven-year-olds, dads, sharing Chiclets, spying on birds, and the impending frog hunt. And I wrote it all down, never to forget the beauty of being there.

"You will be there, won't you, Dad?" he asked, pulling me temporarily away from the newspaper, which I was trying to read before I went over the work I had brought to the living room with me.

"Oh yes, definitely," I said. "I wouldn't miss it."

But I almost did, trying to get one last project completed, one more phone call returned, one more file cleared. Then I dashed out and headed to the park for my kindergartener's first-ever T-ball game.

The year was 1990. Probably the second-busiest year of my adult life.

Patrick sat hunched over on the bench, digging trenches in the soft sand with his new tennis shoes, the sun beating down on the top of his brand-new, navy-blue baseball cap. The Rockets! He was scraped on both elbows, sweaty, and his tight new socks showed dirt from an earlier slide during practice. He was surrounded by a thousand—or at least twelve—very loud, first-time T-ballers.

"Patrick," I said through the chain-link fence. "I'm here."

"Good," he said. "I'm glad you got here before I went up to bat. I'm gonna hit a home run."

He didn't hit a home run, but he did hit the ball off the T, and he did run to the right base, and he didn't run again until he was supposed to. For his first T-ball game, he was doing quite well for himself. In the outfield, he was able to track down the ball pretty well after it went shooting past him, and he threw it relatively close to the pitcher's mound to stop the play. Good arm. Great eye.

I sat with his mom, surrounded by other moms and dads who had decided to put away the demands others place upon them to "be there" for this once-in-a-lifetime occasion. Everybody's son played better than everybody else's.

At the end of the evening, we recounted the day, the spectacular plays, the funny mistakes. Yes, he ran fast. Yes, he threw good.

"Dad?" Patrick asked. "Did we win?"

"Yes, Patrick," I said. "We all won."

I won by being there.

Someday, when I am old and too often alone, I will pull out my valuable collection, and carefully and tenderly polish each piece. All those "being theres" that I have stashed away through the years will have increased in value, keeping me interested in collecting more and more. During the years, I will have shared them often with my children, pulling them out when doubts appeared, using them to close up gaps and heal hurts. There is great power in "remember whens," but you can only use them if you have them.

Most people I know are busy. We all miss things every now and then, but if we miss too much of the everyday, if we pass by too many once-in-a-lifetime moments, we loosen the bonds that tie us to our children.

I am glad to know that someday, when Zachary's son or daughter asks him, "Did your daddy ever lift you up to see inside of a bird's nest?" he will be able to answer. And just in case he forgets, I've written it down.

5

The One to Call On

I t was Saturday morning again, and I was staring down a bowl of Corn Pops while trying to think of all the creative things one can do with a severed telephone cord. And then it rang again. It being the telephone, the curse of Alexander.

"It's for Russell," I predicted. "It's Brittany . . . or Tonya . . . or Julie . . . or . . ."

"It's for you, Dad," Russell said, his eyes rolling to nearly pure white. "Something about the dog getting in the neighbor's trash."

I wanted to lie, to develop chronic pneumonia, to be out working in the garden or gone to the hardware store. Why do I get these calls? What do they presume I am, the head of the house?

Just once, I'd like to get a nice call, like from a radio station telling me I won a cruise to Alaska, or from a lawyer telling me of an inheritance, or from the IRS explaining the mistake they made and the date the refund will arrive. But no, I get calls about naughty dogs and bargains of a lifetime.

Or wrong numbers from people who want to know what in the world I'm doing at John's house.

John must be a swell guy. He's got lots of friends.

The phone rang just as I set it in the cradle—a perfect name for something that constantly squalls.

"Russell, it's for you."

He makes it short. We'd already had this long conversation—or lecture, depending on your perspective—about how sixth-grade girls are not supposed to call boys unless there's a really good reason. The day following the lecture, four girls forgot what their homework assignment was . . . and they all called Russell. The fact that he knew what the assignment was gave an unreal quality to the whole scene. This was a well-planned conspiracy indeed.

No one ever calls me to go play basketball, like they do Zachary; or to invite me to sleep over, like Patrick; or to a birthday party, like Donovan. Even Lauren gets pleasant little calls to remind her to read her Bible story before Sunday.

And Lisa? She moves mountains with Touch-Tone, everything from shifting bank balances to checking computerized messages to verifying homework assignments. And then of course, there's her friend Mary.

Gotta call Mary, she may have moved to the moon since noon.

I don't like the phone. I sound terrible on the voice-mail message. Maybe that's why when I dial in all those codes to check to see who left us a message, I just get to hear various renditions of creative hang-ups.

I must admit that I have used the phone effectively in the past. Ask my wife. Ask her on the phone if you want. I did. That's right, I proposed on the phone. But hey, at least it was long distance.

"Do you really love me?" she asked between tears.

Obviously, the expense of calling long distance did not speak for itself. And so, in unhurried—and expensive—detail, I professed my love for my one and only. How dare she graduate and leave me on that lonely college campus to eat cold pizza all alone in my shabby, silent apartment. Who was I going to do laundry with on Friday nights? Yes, I do love you, and I miss you, and I want to share a telephone number with you for the rest of my life.

Her and the rest of the world it turned out, for now there's seven of us for whom the bell tolls . . . endlessly.

Zachary once worried that coming to know God was a too-serious moment in his life, that once God takes control a man can no longer have fun, because God is not a humorous being, but only a judge who dishes out guilt until we so change our lives that all the fun goes out. Man, Zach said, had so messed up the world God created that God could no longer laugh. And, he explained, every time God got ahold of a man he put him to work trying to straighten out the mess of his forefathers. Laughter took too much time away from the labor of the righteous. Well, he didn't put it in those words, but he made it pretty clear that being a Christian—if you really answer the call—didn't look too cool to him, in retrospect. This forever thing was beginning to look eternal indeed.

And then I told him about the time God called me on the telephone.

Lisa and I were struggling to put out the weekly edition of the small newspaper we had dedicated ourselves to producing. I'd write, she'd sell ads, and we'd optimistically stare at a deadline until it passed and then, with our small, dedicated staff, we'd work well past midnight as the rest of the town, and our children, went to sleep.

We didn't blame each other, we just worked and worked and worked, and vowed that the next week we'd start early and make the deadline. Finally, exhausted, we turned out the lights and headed for home.

We crawled into bed. Shortly, we crawled out. A new day, not an easy one to greet, had begun.

I ate my Corn Pops and headed toward Oklahoma City

and the printer with the pages. Lisa matched children to socks, paper sacks, and spiral notebooks and sent them off to school. Wednesday was her day at home. I was so tired I had no business driving. She was so tired she had no business doing anything.

But we had things to do. We always had things to do. Too many things.

"It's 70 degrees and climbing and the sun is shining. Another beautiful day," said the disc jockey on the car radio. Such a cheery voice for 8:00 a.m. I ignored him.

What I couldn't ignore was the need created by the large Dr Pepper I'd had for breakfast with my Corn Pops. I realized I'd never make it to the city, so I pulled into the rest stop on the interstate just south of town. I'd made little progress, for the rest stop was really just over the hill and only a few miles from our house. You'd think God could have done a tad better job on the bladder thing. Well, at least He'd led someone to invent rest stops on highways.

Lisa, meanwhile, was enjoying herself immensely, practicing a new art form she had perfected: calling utility companies. It was the time of the month when she would sit down and call each one and explain why the payment was late and beg for mercy and one more day of hot water and air conditioning.

What to do . . . what to do. By dawn she had rehearsed various stories and dredged up all kinds of creative excuses. She'd even practiced a few lies before deciding she just couldn't go quite that far. In her exhausted state, she couldn't remember in which pile she'd last put the telephone directory. Instead, she found "Brand X," one of those generic directories put out by clever advertising salespeople. It was notorious for errors.

She looked up the number and started to dial when she realized that Brand X had obviously erred when printing the directory. She knew, for instance, that all Guthrie numbers were preceded by 282. Therefore, the electric company couldn't be 843. In our financial situation, the last thing we needed right now was an accidental long-distance call. Surely, she decided, the number is supposed to have a 282 prefix. She sighed . . . she dialed . . . she waited.

As I stepped from the car, at the rest stop, the piercing brightness of the spring morning hit me and woke me up much more than I wanted to be awakened. It caught me in midyawn and made my eyes water so much that tears went streaming down my cheeks. Then I heard a familiar noise.

I was the only person at the rest stop, and I knew that, but I still looked all around me.

"Somebody answer the phone," I shouted, just like at home.

The phone? Yes, the public pay phone was ringing off the pole. It had to be the wrongest of wrong numbers, but I thought, "Why not?" I walked over to the pay phone, checked again to make sure I was alone, and answered with a flourish.

"Hello?" I said.

Silence. Followed by a shriek.

"Thom! What on earth are you doing at the electric company?"

"Lisa? What on earth are you doing calling the pay phone at the rest stop?"

We went through "you're checking up on me" and "you're never where you say you are" to "I can't believe this" all the way to "this is downright spooky." I expected Rod Serling to come walking out of the restroom to the *Twilight Zone* theme.

Ignorant of my exhaustion, I stayed on the phone and we went from exclamation to conversation. An unhurried, real conversation, without interruption. She told me of her concern about the electric bill and we discussed solutions. I told her to get some sleep. She told me to wear my seat belt and lay off the Dr Pepper.

I didn't want to hang up. We'd shared a wondrous experience, so far beyond probability that we could only suppose that God knew we both needed, more than anything else that morning, each other's voices. He connected us.

When I got back in the car, I turned up the radio, sang aloud with it, and made it all the way to the printer's before I remembered why I stopped at the rest stop in the first place. At home, Lisa called the electric company, visited cheerfully with the customer service person, and told the huge utility how much we appreciated its patience.

When I first told Zach that story, he did what most people do. He laughed. And then he thought about it, and he laughed again.

"See, Zach," I said. "God *does* have a sense of humor. Every time I think life is getting a little too serious, I remember that three-way person-to-person call in the wilderness."

That call was the beginning of a subtle change in our family. We both wondered how we had become so devoted to our work that we could leave our children with a stranger to put them in bed . . . how I could rise in the morning and sit across the table without even saying good morning.

Two years later, we were out of the business that was so dominating our lives and I had a new job . . . with the telephone company. Now, tell me again God doesn't have a sense of humor.

"Hello, Doo-Dad," said Donovan as he answered the phone.

"Hi, Donnie," I said. "How did you know it was me?"

"Because you call every day at this time," he said.

"I do?"

"Yes, and you always ask how school went."

"Oh," I said. "Guess it's a habit."

"That's okay," he said. "'Cause it didn't go too good today."

And then he told me about it, and I listened. And then he listened to me. And we were connected.

6

The Nice, Quiet Neighborhood That Was

We'd moved into a new neighborhood where no one knew who we were . . . or how many we were. One of those nice, quiet neighborhoods where, just before sunset, the retired couples take to the streets in their sneakers and walk around and around the block, admiring each other's flower beds and edged lawns, exchanging transplants from each other's gardens. And then, there we suddenly were, right smack-dab in the middle of a nice, quiet, little neighborhood that was.

We'd been situated only a couple of days. I was in the front yard watering the flower beds—we so wanted them to be admired—when the neighbor to the right came over to introduce himself.

"Thought you might want these back," he said, his arms filled with assorted balls, Frisbees, airplanes, and for some odd reason, the tie I'd worn to church on Sunday. "I found them on my side of the backyard fence. Kinda got yourself some spirited little guys there, don't you?"

"They definitely put the term 'privacy fence' to the test,

I guess," I joked. The neighbor, Wylie, laughed, spat a little tobacco juice near my shoe, and said something about how his wife had always hankered for a trained pit bull dog and this might be the time.

"Just a joke," Wylie said. "Your kids are cute. Send 'em over anytime . . . to clean up the yard."

Again he reminded me he was "just jokin'." Keen sense of humor.

Our neighbor across the street was just crossing into the yard when I realized Donovan had stolen the hose right from under my nose and had trapped the kitten in the maple tree.

"Nice boy," said Leo, a retired gentleman with his hand out. He looked at Donovan, but he wasn't trembling or backing away to the curb. "Reminds me of my grandson."

Leo had brought brownies, which his wife Nita had just taken from the oven.

"She's a little down in her back or she would have brought them over herself," said Leo. "Welcome to the neighborhood. We've been needing some little ones to liven it up."

"You'll have all the life you ever wanted," I said. "I guarantee it."

The afternoon spent itself as I watered and trimmed and Zach mowed and Lisa washed windows and potted a bright red geranium for the front porch. Children wandered in and out, returning from expeditions through the neighborhood.

Later that evening, I suggested to Lisa that we quit trying to accomplish anything and just sit on the front swing and watch the sneakers go by. I was looking forward to getting old so I'd have more energy. Pretty soon, another neighbor from across the street, Gordon, came over and introduced himself and offered to trim the low-hanging branches on the maple. Not long thereafter his wife, Aileen, crossed the street with lemonade and Oreos. Up and down the street, lawn edgers were buzzing and solitary weeds were being plucked here and there, but the busy hands were waving and the faces were smiling. Far in the distance, I could hear the bells of the satisfied ice cream man fading away. He'd discovered us, and he too had dropped by for a visit.

I remembered the many moves I'd endured as a youngster as my family stayed one step ahead of the bill collector. My mother would lay out the well-worn welcome mat, heave a deep sigh, smile, and say, "Bloom where you're planted."

Well, here in this neighborhood, you'd better bloom pretty or someone's going to pluck you.

"You know, we may just like it here," I said to Lisa, waking her up. "There's a lot to be said for neighborhoods like this where it is nice and quiet."

"*Was* nice and quiet," Lisa smiled. And we went in to wrestle the kids into bed.

It didn't take our family long to feel comfortable in our new neighborhood. Lauren and Patrick especially made themselves right at home.

"Are you sure she's not just making a pest of herself?" I asked Lisa one Sunday afternoon as Lauren headed for the front door on her way out into the neighborhood.

"Of course not," Lisa answered. "She's a little blessing."

Right. In disguise.

"Look at her," I said. "She's scary."

Four-year-old Lauren had on her plastic Barbie high heels, a dozen strands of plastic beads around her neck, a bright red shawl over her shoulders, and a big white straw hat with a massive silk flower arrangement sticking out of it. She carried with her her bag.

"She looks beautiful," said Lisa. "And don't you ever say otherwise."

The door banged shut and Lauren disappeared from view, headed next door to visit Georgene. The vision of her loveliness is permanently etched into my brain.

"Where you goin'?" I asked Patrick as he whizzed by.

"To Gordon's," he said. "We're gonna work on my bike."

"Well, don't you drive Gordon crazy with a million questions. And if he acts busy, you come straight back home."

To Patrick and Lauren, all neighbors are fair game. And in our neighborhood, populated by the elderly and retired, there were a lot of easy targets.

The door opened and Lauren came back in, in tears. Georgene hadn't answered the door. Their car was in the driveway and Lauren was sure she heard somebody inside, but no one came to the door when she rang the bell.

Lauren had made a daily habit of visiting Wylie, Georgene, and Georgene's mother, Mabel, a woman with a beautiful spirit in an aging body. Mabel loved Lauren and Lauren loved Mabel. She'd slide up close to the wheelchair and the two would sit quietly together while Georgene played songs on the organ. Then they'd share a snack, play cards—Old Maid or War—and when it appeared Mabel was tiring, Georgene would figure out a way to send Lauren home. Sometimes, if Mabel was sleeping or feeling poorly, Georgene just wouldn't answer the door, pretending they were not at home.

"I know," Lauren brightened. "I'll visit Nita."

Ah, Nita, the keeper of the kitchen. The connoisseur of candy. The purveyor of popcorn. And the lady who always sends Lauren back home with a new hat and a new story about the good old days.

Patrick wandered in a few minutes later.

"I'm going bike riding," he said.

"I thought it was broken," I said.

"Not anymore. Gordon fixed it."

It wasn't until many months had passed that I found out where Patrick was going on his two-wheeled missions. I was sure he wasn't going beyond the prescribed limits, but he always seemed to pedal away with such a sense of urgency and return with such an air of accomplishment.

We learned where he'd been going later—delivering his "mail" to most of our neighbors' houses. He hadn't really learned to write, but he loved to draw those pictures.

"You'll just never know how much Patrick's little gifts have meant to me," Marge, a neighbor from down the street, told Lisa one day. "Every time I would come out to my swing, feeling lonely or tired, there'd be a little surprise and it would just sweep me right out of my blues."

We had not known of Patrick's mailman ministry. He delivered his pieces of art, colorful flowers, special leaves, odd rocks, empty birds' nests, marbles. Almost every day he had placed one special object on Marge's swing or in a neighbor's mailbox or by a door. Its message? Thinking of you.

Gradually, Lisa and I saw our circle of friends in the neighborhood grow. Everyone knew Patrick and everyone wanted to meet Patrick's parents.

As soon as he learned to write, he expanded his "ministry," leaving letters and stories throughout the neighborhood. "Just to make sure people get mail," he explained.

We lived in that neighborhood several years and saw lots of changes. Mabel got better and worse and better again. Overlooking my own neglect of the matter, Wylie taught the boys to fish. Gordon seemed to get older, forgetting people's names but never forgetting how to repair bicycles. Nita cleaned out more closets and added more hats to Lauren's outrageous collection. Trees grew and got trimmed back.

One day, a stretch limo pulled up outside Leo and Nita's house and they came out, he in a tux and she in a sequined gown. Fifty years of marriage. I told the children that someday their mom and I would celebrate such a milestone.

I think we knew we were really a part of the neighborhood when John, a good neighbor down the street who had recently sent his youngest son off to college, put his head together with Charlie, who, having grown up as one of eleven, only shrugged at the notion that five children were a handful. The next day, a big hole appeared next to our driveway. Three hours later, *the* neighborhood basketball goal, having been on that street for two generations, in two different yards, was in mine. For my boys. From their friends.

Life in that nice, quiet neighborhood was as perfect as we had ever known it. Not completely perfect, of course, but better than merely pleasant, to be sure. We laughed a lot there. And cried a little.

"Wylie hates me," I remember Lauren whining as she sat alone on the front porch swing, her head buried between her knees, her long hair hanging in disheveled ringlets.

"Why would you say that?" I asked.

"I killed his tree."

Well, she hadn't actually killed it, just sort of temporarily pared back its potential. Many an early evening I had seen Wylie out examining the green pecans on that tree, salivating over the day when they'd be ripe for picking. He'd spend hours on his front porch chasing away squirrels from his little tree, which was about to yield its first-ever edible crop. Anyone who came walking down the street would be stopped by Wylie to hear how he had planted the little seedling five years before and had waited patiently for the day when he'd harvest his first delicious pecans.

Unbeknown to Wylie, another little seedling had been planted almost five years before. Lauren. And unbeknown to Wylie, Lauren, more clever perhaps than all the squirrels in the neighborhood, had taken a footstool from the garage and carefully stripped every green pecan from the tree, tossing them into the water-filled street gutter where they slowly turned the water green as they prepared to rot.

"Wylie hates me," she had moaned. And I thought she might be right.

But of course, Wylie didn't hate Lauren. He was sixty-five and could easily wait until he was sixty-six to eat a homemade, home-grown pecan pie.

I will never forget those years on Chaucer Street. I will remember them because of the love and acceptance the people showed us, the changes we all shared with each other, the good things that were done and said, the good cooking, and the beautiful flowers. But I will remember Chaucer Street best because it was where Patrick and Lauren learned to be neighbors. And reminded us all to do the same.

7

Explore the Distant Shore

"*A*ll dads camp with their sons," Zachary had told me back in February. "*All.*"

Standing behind him with their hands on their hips were Patrick, Donovan, Russell, and Lauren. All dads camp with their daughters too, I suppose.

Zachary's complaint came each February, hailing the eternal hope of another spring and summer on the horizon. Since I'd promised him a camping trip back when he was five and had never fulfilled that promise, I had to admire his perseverance . . . once again. Why are people in my family so persevering?

This year, I would join the dads of the world. I would camp with my sons. Correction: Lisa and I and Patrick and Lauren would sleep in a nice, little air-conditioned cabin. The other boys could pitch the tent out behind the cabin. A promise tinged with compromise.

First, I had to come to grips with reality. For thirty years I'd rebelled against camping. I love the outdoors, the feel of the wind, the smells of the flowers, the butterflies, birds, squirrels, riverbanks, lapping lakes, starlit nights. But no one taught me how to camp. It is not true, Zachary, that *all* dads camp with their sons. I know.

We began by spreading out dozens of brochures and maps. Every place seemed ripe for invasion. They all had trees and water. We eventually focused on Lake Murray, a resort in southern Oklahoma visited by 1.5 million people a year. Since a third are from out of state, that narrowed our chances of ever running into any of them again . . . just in case they didn't want to run into us.

"That's it," I announced. "We're going camping."

I plodded through the work days with adventure on my mind and dread in my heart. Finally, C-Day dawned.

"I hope they have a convenience store near the park," Lisa said as we got into the van. "The kids are counting on s'mores over the campfire. The marshmallows probably survived your packing, but you ground the graham crackers into bird feed when you slammed the van's back door, and those chocolate bars will probably melt because you didn't get them into the cooler in time."

I accepted the blame silently. We'll give the birds the smashed graham crackers and they'll stop eating bugs, and the bugs will eat us up. And if the Hershey bars do melt back there, it'll probably be on my pillow. Plus, there's bound to be a "convenience" store, though the word has no meaning to this family.

All five kids carried small suitcases, bags, or satchels filled with their own ideas of what might be needed on a three-night camping trip. Everything from Lauren's Barbie flashlight to Russell's drawing pads and pencils. Zachary had a knife for killing snakes. And there were secret things. *Lots* of secret things.

By the time we reached the interstate, we were singing songs in the car, turning "Old McDonald Had a Farm" into a rap tune.

All the while, unbeknown to me, Russell had his tape

recorder going. I found out late that night—about midnight—
when I went out to make a final check on the boys. By then,
the exhausted campers in the next tent had crawled further
into their sleeping bags to escape the strains of the Hunters
warbling out over a cheap speaker powered by dying batteries.

The overpowering abundance of stars twinkled like city
dwellers dream they do. An owl's hoot highlighted the otherwise silent night. A few laughing campers in the distance
provided the only other sound. I was surrounded by too much
beauty to go inside, for I knew the wildest inventions of sleep
could not compare.

The same wind that rattled the screens at home rustled
softly through the leaves above, and I leaned against a tree
cushioned by growth I was thankful I would never have to
trim. In darkness, the world around me was beautifully rug-
ged, and the shadows created by the moon danced and kept
me company, even as I soaked up energy from solitude.

Here and there, gray smoke drifted into the sky as
campfires were doused and campers turned in for the night.
I was reminded that there is more than the mind and the
soul, and though they were being enriched, I was ready to
put my body to bed.

Before leaving the boys alone in the glorious darkness,
I checked the zipper on the tent. Peeking in, I found that
Zachary and Russell had rolled to the center, sandwiching
Donovan in between. Their breathing was a chorus of peace,
so I paused, prayed, turned, and tiptoed toward the cabin.

"Dad?" came a little voice from the wilderness. "I
gotta go."

Obviously I *had* neglected my boys. Even I knew enough
about camping trips to know that when you gotta go, you just
go. We were surrounded by trees. Quickly, this crisis was
behind us. Our first day was a success.

The next morning was Saturday. Naturally I overslept,
unaware that such a thing can be done on a camping trip.
What did I miss, a breakfast meeting with a butterfly? Out-

side the cabin, Lisa was tending the campfire, the last piece of sausage slowly shriveling up as the children prepared to cast lots for it. A little voice of survival deep inside me propelled me out of the cabin to claim my morning grub.

It was 7:00 a.m. Do you know where my children were? Lined up on a log, shoes tied, hair combed, bellies full, backpacks at the ready. The question was, ready for what?

"Hurry up and eat, Dad," said Zachary. "We want to hike the nature trail while it's still cool."

Cool? The sun was barely up and it was 95 degrees in the shade. Our cabin was just across from the Buckhorn Nature Trail. Lauren stayed with Mom. She'd seen all the nature she needed when a spider crawled out of a crack in the log she was sitting on.

"Only one requirement or I'm not going," I said. "From beetles to butterflies, snakes to turtles, we have to find every color of the Crayola deluxe box. And the sky and the trees don't count."

Thus challenged, they discovered nature everywhere. This was no mere hike down a nature trail, this was an eyes-wide-open learning experience in God's creation.

"I don't know what it is," Patrick said. "But I've found it."

"It's a deteriorated soft drink can," I said sadly. "Put it in your backpack."

I lectured the boys on how a nature trail remains a nature trail only if man takes nothing in and takes nothing out. A black snake slithered away in agreement as green frogs jumped and brown turtles buried themselves in the cool mud of a slow-moving stream.

Small plants of every shape and every imaginable shade of green, some topped with wild, beautiful flowers, grew in the still moisture far below the trees. A beautiful butterfly struggled in vain, captured by the silky stickiness of a dewy web.

"Look what I found," said Donovan in hushed excitement. "All laid out like he was gettin' dressed for church."

And there, just to the side of the trail, was the skull, shell, and inner bones of a small turtle that had been devoured by something bigger, something which may now have already been eaten elsewhere, adding another link to the food chain.

The trail ended at the lake's edge. Watching the waves lap the shore was so peaceful I almost forgot I had four boys with me. Four boys normally so loud—so normal—but now, staring out at dancing water, just like me. Even when they began skipping flat rocks on the water's surface, they did it quietly, almost reverently. God, when He created all this beauty, created such overwhelming respect for it that it grabbed us and left us speechless.

On the return hike, I tried to ignore my tightening leg muscles, the sweat dripping from my brow, and the fact I was now carrying two extra backpacks. We were thirsty and hungry and enlightened.

The day flashed by and the required wiener roast was under way. The coat hangers were wimpy and an occasional wienie slipped to its doom in the coals. Short arms gave it their best shot, but even with their faces turned away from the fire, it was just too hot for the kids, so Lisa and I took turns roasting and we ate in shifts. My children ate pork and beans straight from the can. How macho.

Then came the s'mores. The marshmallows that emerged from the flames not completely black were smashed between Hershey squares and newly purchased graham crackers. Lauren burst into tears when she lost her s'more, but joined the laughter when we saw that Russell had sat on it and was stuck to his tree-stump perch.

"Want s'more, Russell?" Lisa asked.

With no dishes to do, we trekked to the tennis courts. Zachary had finally relaxed his restrictions and allowed that tennis could be a part of a camping trip. We laughed and volleyed under the lights till nearly midnight. No one won. No one lost. Most didn't hit the ball.

That night we all slept like rocks on a placid lake, waking to energize our sore muscles with scrambled eggs and cinnamon rolls. It was Father's Day. I was finally going to get to see what they'd smuggled into the van in their backpacks. From Zachary, a notebook for writing more stories about my children—a sign that the embarrassment he suffers is bearable. From Patrick, a Lego hook on a string I could borrow for opening my desk drawers at the office. From Donovan, a pencil sharpener in the shape of an Indian's head, hastily purchased in the lodge souvenir shop. It would come in handy working together on homework problems. From Russell, money . . . to take him to play video games. From Lauren—a kiss.

Here, where we had all spent this time together, I got the message loud and clear: more of the same, Dad. Every gift they had given me was something I could use with them.

In my book, every moment of this trip had been absolutely wonderful. From the back-against-the-wall promise to the final s'more, it was blessed. But there was something I knew I had to take care of.

I called Zach aside and we headed down the Buckhorn Trail.

"Zachary," I said, "I really am sorry I didn't take you camping eight years ago. I should have, partly because I promised and mainly because you had your heart set on it then as much as you always have. But I think you've known the truth for a while, and that's that I just never *wanted* to go.

"I waited all this time, never realizing how much I'd love it. From sunrise to sunburn, it's been great. And even though I'm glad all of us were here, I can't help wishing I'd taken that first little trip back when you wanted it so bad. I was just afraid back then that I'd really mess it up and you'd be disappointed."

"That's okay," Zach said unconvincingly and then went

on. "You did everything fine. You just did it late. This was supposed to be my camping trip. You promised it to me when I was a little kid and I didn't get it. Now, they're all little kids, and they're getting it. It just doesn't seem fair. That's all."

This sudden honest expression, brought on by common-sense thinking and accurate guilt placement, was a new revelation from Zachary. Something very teenagerish. Still, what he was expressing was very childlike, and that was comforting.

"What's dumb is that I'm glad they were all here," he said. "I was so mad that my dumb brothers and sister were tagging along on my camping trip, but they were kinda fun. And I'm glad they had fun. But, if I was as big a pain when I was five as Lauren is now, no wonder you didn't want to go. Just kidding."

I punched him on his sunburned shoulder and he chased me back to the campsite. We joined the family and sat around drinking soft drinks and telling spooky stories as the sun went down. Not spooky enough apparently, as heads began to nod and yawns began to spread. They were all asleep before bedtime prayers could be said, but I felt confident my praise beneath the trees was felt familywide.

Lisa and I stayed up and shared the shadows. A clear sky dazzled us with stars that wouldn't be so plentiful through the hazy streetlights of Monday.

"This was a good idea I had," I said.

"Zach had," she corrected.

And then we started telling stories and giggling and laughing out loud. The forest does that to its creatures. Who knows? Maybe birds and bees and butterflies and turtles laugh. Snakes probably snicker. I wonder if Donovan ever heard a fish giggle.

It was a nice, long night and a bright, clear morning. Closely packed together in a crowded van, we went back home . . . where we live.

I believe children's lives are built on "I've been theres" and "I've done thats." If I'm right, we did a lot of building on the eight-year-delayed adventure.

Sunrise and moonlight, no charge.

8

Sharing the Stage

Every daddy's nightmare: A son who's just like him. I had been told it was a father's dream, but then I had four sons, and one of them—everyone says—turned out to be like me.

"But," I argued, "he's more talented. More confident. More coordinated. Better-looking, for sure. And he's certainly harder to get along with. I think he may even be a bit spoiled."

"Then he's like you," Lisa said.

So it was with timid trepidation that I agreed to "co-star" with Russell in the Village Baptist Church Living Christmas Tree production.

In the musical, Russell played me as a child . . . and I played him as an adult. What could be more appropriate for a father and son who are supposed to be so much alike? Of course, I knew if he played me and I played him, there was at least a fifty-fifty chance we'd reach the point where we would kill each other on stage, which would, in effect, be double suicide. Beneath a choir-crowded Christmas tree, and in the spotlight, that could be very dramatic.

On the very first night of rehearsals, eleven-year-old Russell announced to the director, with his usual bravado, that he was ready to do his scenes without a script. (This child is not me.)

"In the sixth month, God sent the angel Gabriel to Nazareth, a town in Galilee, to a virgin pledged to be married . . ."

As I listened to Russell that night, I realized what I had perceived as cockiness was confidence. What I had perceived as "showy" was hard work and preparation. What I had perceived as a desire for the spotlight was a child's open willingness to tell the Christmas story. I looked at my son and realized there was a lot more to see than I had been allowing myself to see.

The director clapped when Russell finished, told me to work hard on my memorization, and rehearsal number one was over.

"You were great," I told Russell over a cold Barq's root beer in the Circle K convenience store parking lot.

"You too," he said, with a perfectly timed burp. "*Not!*"

That night, after Russell crammed his baseball cards under his bed and climbed beneath the covers, I told him good night and sat on the stairs outside his bedroom.

"But the angel said to them 'Do not be afraid. I bring you good news of great joy . . .' "

And that's how he fell asleep, practicing those lines, putting feeling into it, making graceful hand gestures above his bed, maybe even seeing angels.

I sat alone in the living room, resisting the impulse to turn on the television, and listened to my wife recover the house from the clutter of five young children. And I thought of Christmases past.

What was it like when I was Russell's age, eleven? Years fell away until my mind found 1965. And when that year popped into my head, I felt a twinge in my heart. We all have special Christmases we will never let slip from among our most precious memories. I have a couple.

It was two days before Christmas. Our plain one-bedroom apartment was decorated with paper chains of red and green construction paper and pages torn from coloring books and plastered on the walls. The boxes of ornaments and lights and garland had been brought out of the closet days ago and placed in the corner of the living room where the tree would go. But, no tree.

We were children, and try as hard as we might, we couldn't resist whining about the lack of a Christmas tree every time my mother came home from work.

"Everybody's got a tree," I said to my mother. And it was true, for the row of apartments across from ours had a tree in every living room window. Only ours was dark and empty.

"Well, we better do something about that," she said. As I look back, I know now that the smile she was wearing was one of uncertainty. It became more familiar to me through the years as we struggled to pay for the necessities of life. Like Christmas trees.

Since we didn't own a working car at the time, we walked the short block to the Safeway store to find our tree. Two days before Christmas, the pickin's are slim.

"I think it's beautiful," Mother glowed. "When we get it home and get all the decorations on . . . and put that side against the wall, we'll say what we say every year."

"That it's the prettiest one ever?" asked Sue.

We didn't say that. We were raised to be too honest. The tree had several gaps in it and it leaned. It fell over before we could even get it decorated. Mom, ever resourceful, took some kite string, thumbtacked each end to the wall and allowed the tree to lean against the string for support. No way. It fell, sending already-dry needles flying.

Trying not to look flustered, she took a hammer and nails and actually nailed the stand to the hardwood apartment floor. Personally, I think she was overestimating the landlord's Christmas spirit a bit, but she was desperate. We had to get that tree decorated before Christmas Eve.

On went the decorations, treasures from Christmases past and new treasures from school classrooms. And she was right, well-decorated, it was kinda pretty. But it still leaned.

We stood back, hot chocolate in hand, and admired the tree from every angle. Slowly it began to tilt, the back of the stand lifting off the floor . . . gracefully, in slow motion, it moved from perpendicular to parallel, sending remnants of Christmases past flying and shattering on the hardwood floor.

In the wink of an eye, Mother unplugged the lights, jerked the stand, bent nails and all, out of the floor, grabbed the tree by the trunk through one of its many bare spots, and headed out the door, across the parking lot, down the street and straight for the Safeway, balls shattering, icicles flying, light cords tangling in the dry leaves littering the street gutters.

"Mother," I shrieked. "Please don't!"

I remember thinking every one of my classmates would be in the checkout line, pointing at the crazy woman doing a Grinch number with the ugliest Christmas tree in town.

All the stress and strain of a long year came flowing out of Mother as she tried to explain to the manager of Safeway that her children would not have a Christmas this year because he was selling defective trees at inflated prices. She looked somewhat like a contestant on *Queen for a Day* trying to convince the judges that she had the worst life of all women and therefore greatly deserved the automatic washing machine.

The grocery store went on automatic pilot as every checker in the place paused to see what their boss would do for this poor hysterical lady and her stunned children hiding behind her coat.

The new tree—with a wonderfully straight trunk and all the new decorations—was beautiful. And the box of candy, offered free and in true Christmas spirit by the teary-eyed checkers, was the best we'd ever had. We put the icicles on one at a time, and I sat beneath the tree and celebrated one of my own Christmas traditions, finger-swinging from one icicle to the next, from branch to branch, yodeling in true Tarzan fashion, all without worry that Christmas would come crashing down upon me.

My big Christmas gifts that year? Chinese checkers, abundant joy, and a clearer sense of being loved. I realized that night that my mother would go through anything, including public humiliation, to meet my needs and satisfy my longings.

Twenty-six years later I was about to go through public humiliation myself if I didn't learn those lines. However, with Russell as a persistent coach, I was bound to be a success. He'd allow nothing less.

"You can do it, Dad," he told me every time I forgot my line in practice. "It's Christmas!"

And then we'd head home in the cold, crisp night and stop, not for hot chocolate, but for that cold root beer. In his room, quietly above the even breathing of his sleeping brothers, he'd recite and rehearse until sleep stilled him. And I would listen, and remember back . . .

. . . to Russell's first Christmas. We knew he was sick, we just weren't sure how sick. He seemed so small and weak those first four months as he recovered from a severe intolerance to galactose, the sugar in milk. I remembered his mother's tears when the doctor explained her breast milk was keeping him from developing . . . and that routine tests taken shortly after birth showed he might be mentally handicapped or have various physical problems. Because we'd moved to Oklahoma almost immediately after he was born in a small Texas hospital, it had taken weeks for the hospital to track us down. Dangerous weeks for Russell.

When Lisa got the news, she cried and held him tight. She had sensed that something was wrong, but her friends had assured her that she had just forgotten what a tiny baby was like. But she hadn't, and she had known all along that something was wrong with her Russell. He slept too much. He cried too much. He had too little energy.

Only time would tell. And now it was Christmas and we were watching for signs of developing muscle tone prompted by special formulas.

On Christmas morning, two-and-a-half-year-old Zachary kept unwrapping baby Russell's presents and piling them around him. Tiny Russell just slept on. I remember the frustrations of taking pictures, finally saying to Lisa, "I don't know. I think he's smiling, don't you?" and then snapping away. Eleven years later I see in those photos the faintest of smiles, almost like he knew something I did not.

By his second Christmas, Russell's weakness was a thing of the past. Russell was tearing the packages wide open and there was another baby boy sleeping under the tree. All three were "all boy." Almost too much boy.

I pushed aside the memories and kissed the sleeping thespian on the cheek. He turned toward the wall and smiled and mumbled, probably some line from the musical.

The rehearsals flew by and I rose to the challenge Russell's natural stage presence created. I memorized. I gestured. I dredged up feeling. I worked hard. And he helped me.

And we drank a lot of root beer and laughed more than we knew we could and talked about great Christmases, brothers and sisters, rookie cards and fears and doubts and hopes and dreams. I think he was glad to know I still have them.

It was a Christmas present I never expected. For that Christmas I learned that—no matter what anyone says—Russell is not like me. Russell is Russell, just like Zach is Zach, Donovan is Donovan, Patrick is Patrick, and Lauren is Lauren.

And eggnog is not the drink of Christmas. Not for me and Russell, anyway. It's a cold Barq's root beer . . . preferably in the parking lot of the Circle K.

9
Solid and Sturdy

It was one of the first pieces of furniture Lisa's parents bought after they married. The young couple had just graduated from the University of Texas. Bill was a second lieutenant in the Air Force and Vaudine was a new bride.

"Our family," he said, "will share much more than food around this table." And it became the center of their home, where friends and family would come to share coffee and sorrow, pies and happiness.

Lisa and her brother Ken cut their teeth on its corners. So, when we moved it into our house, her dad talked as if another child had gone away to college. I kept wanting to say, "Bill, it's only a table," but I didn't want to diminish the significance he placed on this hinged slab of oak with one leaf and four matching chairs.

"It's still solid and sturdy, after all these years," he told me as he stood back and admired it in our tiny little dining room. He looked as if he'd cry. I came very close again to saying, "Hey, Bill, it's a table . . . a creative tree," but I held my tongue.

Lisa and I had been married two years, and I was not about to question the emotional involvement of my only father-in-law. If he'd wanted to build a monument to his dining room table, I'd have gone right out to gather the stones and mix up the mortar.

I remember how he ran his hands along the smooth edge of the table's top, feeling for nicks in the wood. He'd sanded it and stained it and presented it to Lisa as a gift. No special occasion, he said, just a little something from their home to ours. "It will be perfect for your growing little family."

Considering we were still in the beanbag stage of home furnishings, real wood looked awfully nice. Finally, something on which to display the silver candelabra we'd received from one of her more practical aunts.

"Never know when you might need to entertain," she'd said, as she'd mosied through the reception line with a handkerchief to her cheek. Right, we'll put it next to the pizza pans, another entertainment essential.

Anyway, the table had been in Bill's warehouse for about five years. It showed the nicks and stains of years of use. A coat of white enamel paint had replaced the natural wood stain. Lisa's mother had painted it so it would look new, back before they could afford a big dining table.

But it was like new again, returned to its natural wood color, when Lisa and I placed our first pizza on it and pulled Zachary up in his matching wooden highchair and said grace. He quickly spilled his milk, splattering it across the top of the table and into the pizza. The table was suitably commissioned for a new generation of service.

That was fourteen years ago.

"Guys, wash your hands and bring in the chairs," I yelled. "It's time to eat."

Lauren came rolling by in the chair that, when we're not eating, serves at the computer. She paused and, without words, conveyed her disgust that once again I had failed to take notice of her femininity.

"Okay," I apologized. "Guys *and* girls."

From every doorway they came, upstairs and down, dragging a mix-match of chairs, including the footstool from the living room.

Now we sit we down to eat. I pray the Lord to still our feet.

"Dear Lord," I prayed. "Thank You for our many blessings. Thank You for a beautiful day. Thank You for teachers and schools and jobs and for letting us learn and work. Thank You for time to play and relax. Help us to live lives that make a difference, lives that show others that Jesus lives in us. And Lord, we thank You for this food. In Jesus' name. Amen."

I might as well have said "attack," for that's what they did. First the bread, then the meat. They ignored the carrots, which is just as well, for Lisa can serve those with one hand and remove extra rolls from plates with the other, issuing her familiar stern warning about eating vegetables first.

Family counselors, in newspaper and magazine articles, issue grave warnings that society's impending breakdown is due in part to the fact that American families too rarely gather at the dinner table. They say more and more families are eating on the run, meeting at fast-food restaurants between ball games and dance lessons, or skipping meals entirely to go to meetings or to work late. These writers claim to be writing about the "average" American family, which is not something we've ever worried about being labeled as.

I looked around me. Seven people, each, yes each, bigger than the day before, crowded around a table that is just too small. It's a valiant little table, but this was just never meant to be.

Everyone was trying to be peaceful. After all, the prayer had barely vanished from my lips. Then things began to deteriorate.

Patrick accidentally kicked Donovan under the table. Granted, it looks like an octopus convention under there, but we have all been instructed from the day we graduate from the highchair to place our feet under our chairs—and keep them there.

Lauren was a little overzealous in her refusal to eat broccoli, waving her arms in front of her and making upchuck sounds. Russell, yelling "She's grossing me out," was a little too physical in shoving her arms away from his carefully staked out territory. His tumbler tumbled, dousing his plate and coming to rest in his lap.

Zachary laughed, which made Russell mad enough to throw his bread, which he did, sending it skimming through a massive puddle of ketchup on Zachary's plate. Then Zachary yelled, and I, even though I know better, laughed, which set Lisa to glaring. Which pretty much stopped the action altogether.

"Can we please try again?" she asked, in a voice that made it clear the alternative was a two-week pass to Siberia. I felt the chill already.

We composed ourselves, scooted all the bodies back to the table, stuck our feet beneath our chairs, and began to discuss the day's events. We began with the obligatory "guess what I read in the paper today?" segment wherein I make sure the children are somewhat familiar with the rapidly changing course of events defining the world they are to inherit.

This segment is usually followed by complaints from everyone about the general behavior of humans. That runs the gamut from the man who ran the red light while reading a newspaper and eating an ice cream cone to the teacher who wouldn't issue a hall pass no matter how tightly Patrick crossed his legs and jumped up and down.

Then we settle into the cruelty-of-life segment where everybody argues that he or she has the greatest academic load, and of course, I make it clear that I work harder than anyone, just to make sure they can purchase pencils with which to work their academic miracles.

"Lucky Mom," said Russell. "She gets to stay home all day and do what she wants."

I headed Lisa off at the pass, quickly enumerating the many things she does all day, in addition to getting five children to school in clean clothes and with lunches and bringing them back to a clean house and a waiting dinner, after which they pass their evenings and then crawl in between clean sheets to gather strength for another assault the next morning.

Soon, we've unwound enough to embrace the possibility that there is good in the world. When that happens, we shift into possibilities. Here we talk of things we might want to do tonight and slowly escalate to dreaming of what we might very well do with the rest of our lives.

Patrick and Lauren squirm in their seats, fighting for entrance into the conversation.

"Let's listen to Lauren," Lisa says, and we all paste an expression of interest on our faces as she rambles through a playground story that seemingly goes nowhere but pleases her immensely for all the attention she has claimed.

The pitch rises as stories get wilder and wilder and imaginations stretch. And everyone gets to practice listening. Eventually, someone yawns and stretches and dismisses himself and the din fades away until Lisa and I are there alone to discuss between us whatever revelations were made by our children. We have practiced the etiquette of self-education. I wonder how parents who do not sit down and eat with their chidren every day keep up with what's going on in their lives.

When I was ten, we had a nice, big formica-topped dining table. My mother sat at one end, my stepfather at the other, my brother and I on one side, my two sisters on the other. And we passed the potatoes and the peas, and the ketchup, which my stepfather watered down to make it last. And we drank our water or our milk and we sat up straight and quiet. When we finished our meal, we placed our silverware across our plates and waited to be noticed. Eventually, my stepfather would glance toward me and I would say, "May I be excused?" "Yes, you may," he would say, and the meal would end.

Meals were a solemn occasion. Being children, we were left to make what fun we could of them by whispering crude remarks about the food to each other when he was distracted. Sue, my nine-year-old sister, would giggle, then I'd giggle and if we were successful, one or both of us would be sent from the table.

At least once a week we had lima beans, which we called "slima beans." I could tell they were on the menu because Sue would take her bath before dinner and line her housecoat pockets with plastic sandwich wrap. My job, as caring brother, was to distract my stepfather so she could place her beans, a spoonful at a time, in her housecoat, to be flushed away after dinner.

By the time they were teenagers, our older brother and sister found plenty of excuses not to be around for dinner.

A few years ago, Lisa and I did a little dreaming and made a list of things we wanted. Clothes. A vacation. College savings. We'd been to some friends' house for dinner and marveled at the roominess of their large dining table. Had we no manners we could even have put our elbows on the table, there was so much room.

So, a new dining table went on the top of our priority list. After all, this old table, purchased by her parents as newlyweds, was never intended to seat more than four people.

"It would make a great hobby table," I suggested. "The kids could build models on it."

But somehow, we just never made it to the furniture store. Every morning and every evening, the familiar cry still goes out: "Bring in the chairs."

This little dining table is our courtroom, our bulletin board, our public address system, our classroom, our lecture hall. We knock knees and rub elbows and spill things on each other. It's where we cry over spilt milk—literally—and every other thing worth crying over.

Quite often now, we put eight chairs at the table, one for whoever happened to be in our home long enough for a meal to be set. It may be small, but we've put a lot out on the table and it always holds up strong. Still solid and sturdy after all these years.

One night, as I sat at that very table sorting food coupons while Lisa sat across from me sorting bills, my mind wandered. I thought of all the changes my children go through every day, events that challenge them to make choices, draining their mental and physical energies. They need something that doesn't change. A place where they can safely test their ideas and promote their dreams, where they can wrap themselves inconspicuously in the cocoon of the family, where there's an audience for them to parade in front of.

Bring in the chairs. Here we have the table. Solid and sturdy.

Something to be welcomed to, not just excused from.

10

In the Beginning

I n the beginning was the laundry. In that corner. In this
corner. On the couch. On the bed. In the garage. Here,
there, and everywhere. Solids, prints, prewashed, cold
only, wrinkle-resistant. You name it, it's there.

Planning to watch TV? Here, have a basket of clothes
to fold. Heading out to the garage? Here, put these in the
washer, will you? Headed upstairs? Please bring down the
hamper. Wherever you're going, whatever you're doing, some
towels and T-shirts are going your way.

"I need a shirt."

"Look over by the brown chair."

"I need some underwear."

"Sorry. Still in the dryer."

"Have you seen my baseball pants?"

"They're scheduled for the next load."

"My socks. I've got to have my socks."

"The washer ate them."

I remember when Lisa would spend half an afternoon
hanging diapers out on the clothesline when we lived in the

country. She'd stretch them all out in a neat row and call me to the door to see her handiwork.

"He needs one now," I said. That was an ominous beginning, for whatever is dirty, whatever is wet, whatever is down on the bottom of the pile, is what is needed now.

It is amazing how attached we are to clothes. It's even more amazing how attached we get to clothes when all the towels are dirty and we can't wrap ourselves up to go on a pile-to-pile search for something in our size.

Once Donovan—whose devotion to his little, yellow blankie is legendary—spent a full hour standing under the clothesline on a hot summer day with one thumb poked through one of the knitted holes in the blanket and plugged into his mouth. I wasn't sure if his legs would last until the sun finally dried the blanket and his mother came to remove the clothesline pins and set him free.

Now he waits for more important things, like clean underwear.

"What do you do all day?" I ask as she brings pile after pile of laundry to me every time I sit down. Personally, I think it's a waste of time to fold clothes anyway, when recycling works so well. Pick it up out of a pile, put it on, pull it off, and toss it in a pile. And try to keep the clean piles separate from the dirty one. No problem.

Occasionally though, just grabbing your clothes out of a pile can be dangerous. Just ask Patrick.

It was a Monday, of course. Patrick, in a hurry to get to school on time, grabbed his favorite blue sweatshirt, threw on his jacket, and ran out to the van. Where he waited for Donovan, who was searching for socks; Russell, who was on a mission to find his favorite jeans; and Lauren, who was distraught because her best bow unraveled in the "ravage cycle" of the washing machine. Lisa slipped into some sweat pants she found in a basket by the dining room, and they were off.

All morning long Patrick pulled and tugged on his shirt sleeve, wondering what in the world his mother had done to his favorite sweats. On the playground, standing in the middle of his classmates, he finally couldn't take it anymore.

"Hold on," he said, and everyone stopped to wait. Slowly, Patrick reached way up inside his sleeve and corrected his problem by pulling out a silky pair of his mommy's panties.

A lesser child would have died of embarrassment, but Patrick paraded in his good fortune, milking all the attention he could, waving the panties for his classmates to see before he finally walked over to his teacher and asked to be excused to take them back to the room.

"A spare pair," he said. "Just in case I need them."

Actually, Lisa probably needed them. There was at least a 75-percent chance it was her only clean, unburied pair.

Our life as a maried couple with five children is marked with circumstances, fortunate and otherwise. One of the otherwise was the apparent demise of our washing machine, one of Lisa's dearest and most confidential friends.

I came home from work to find her in her ugliest knee socks, near tears, sitting in the laundry room surrounded by all five laundry baskets, an empty detergent cup sitting dejectedly on the corner of the washing machine.

"Help," she said. "Fix it."

Give her a good humor award. The last time I fixed a machine, it was so confused about its purpose it got up and walked out of the house in the middle of the night.

So, I went out into the laundry room after supper, took a Phillips screwdriver, and made a bunch of banging noises. Then I came back in.

"Guess you better load the van with the first thousand pieces of laundry and head to Mary's," I said. "That machine can't be fixed by a mere mortal. It'll take the strength of ten ordinary men just to get the front panel off."

I slept great that night, not even aware that Lisa stayed up most of the night studying the *Reader's Digest* home-repair manual. Boy, did she ever have a bee in her well-soiled bonnet.

Three times I tried to call home the next morning. Got a busy signal every time. Only later did I find out she was on the line pumping secrets from the most brilliant plumbers and appliance repairmen in town. By asking a different question of each one, she was amassing a pretty detailed description of all the fatal washing machine diseases and all possible cures.

By the time I got home, Lisa had taken the machine apart, strewn its insides all over the laundry room floor, and was beginning to cry.

"That thingamajig," she said, pointing to a little odd-shaped piece. "It won't let go of my water filter."

"Hmmph," I said. "How dare it."

The thingamajig turned out to be no match for Lisa with a hammer—the only tool the kids had not arranged in the back yard to test the properties of rust—and needle-nosed pliers, borrowed from Mary's well-organized garage. Two days had passed, she had consulted with the greatest engineering minds, and the machine was fixed. No parts. No labor. Well, no labor costs.

I was so impressed, I folded eighteen loads of laundry in just under five hours. Just to show my appreciation for matching socks.

We are a partnership, so, about a year later, when the dryer checked it in for a last spin, I went right to work. I unplugged that sucker and dismantled it and sorted through the parts and was about to rewrite my dismal all-thumbs history.

Then Lisa spoiled all my fun when she came out and threw the breaker switch.

"That happens sometimes," she said. "Guess we've got an overload somewhere. Still, wasn't it fun to take it apart?"

I guess it was. And I hopped to and put it right back together. I did my best. For some odd reason, it won't turn off anymore when you open the door, but then we hardly ever turn it off anyway.

It may seem odd, but I take great comfort in a warm load of fresh, clean clothes. I take pride in a tall pile of folded T-shirts. I don't mind folding any of it, but I won't match socks. That's a misnomer.

When I sit on the couch, crowded in by the piles of colors that define my family, I feel security. This is a part of my provision for them. I'm sure Lisa feels love when she dumps in the Tide and rejoices every time she discovers someone left a crayon in a pocket and it made it into the dryer.

A few minutes ago, Russell came by in a shirt that was once Zachary's; Donovan slipped into an old pair of Russell's pants; Patrick pulled on one of Donovan's old sweatshirts; and Zachary headed out the door to basketball practice with my best white socks.

I started to stop him, but the dryer buzzer went off and I just naturally responded to my call. There's a lot of fabric knitting this family together. I gotta keep up.

11

In the Spirit of Compromise

I t was an awesome experience. The world came that close to being totally destroyed, annihilated by nuclear warfare and then further ravaged by rampaging robots. I love science fiction. It's so much like home.

Zach had pleaded with me for weeks to take him to that movie. He took out the trash without being asked. He did his homework right after school. He ate his cabbage without grimace. He even loaded the dishes into the dishwasher without argument.

"Please take me, Dad," he pleaded. "Everybody at school has already seen it. And they say it's awesome. I know you like science-fiction movies. You told me."

He was right. I do like science-fiction movies. And he was right. It was awesome. It was also rated R. And I took him.

The theater was packed with kids, some as young as six or seven. They cheered when cars went flying off the bridges. They oohed when the creature from the future adjusted his molecular structure and pretended to be human. They gasped when a man was impaled on a wall. But they took it all in. And so did Zach. And so did I. It was action unequaled.

We'd had a long discussion before we decided to go see the movie.

"Dad, I *am* thirteen," he said, rolling his eyes. "Plus, the guys at school say it got an R just because of a little blood and guts and maybe a little bad language. But there's no sex or anything."

"I don't know, Zach," I said. "It *is* rated R."

"But everybody's seen it and they're not all psychotic, running around killing people or having nightmares or anything," he said sarcastically. "Besides, I bet there's nothing in this movie I couldn't see just by turning on the television."

"All right," I said. "I'll compromise. I'll take you, but if it's too offensive, we'll get up and walk out. No questions asked."

So we went. And it was a thriller. We didn't walk out, we sat there mesmerized in front of the huge screen as vehicles and buildings exploded and people threw each other around and a little boy was terrorized . . . all in the good name of exciting entertainment.

Lisa hadn't wanted us to go. She didn't accept my argument that Zach was mature enough, that he deserved to be treated differently than his younger siblings, that I would be able use the lesser moral values shown in the movie to illustrate to him that our own family values are more acceptable.

"That's a cop-out," she said.

When we got home, I sort of sanitized the plot and told Lisa it wasn't all that bad. She looked doubtful but let it slide. She could tell I felt guilty about taking Zach. Guilt is a sure sign of a parental slip-up.

A month passed.

"Dad," Zach said, "there's this awesome movie that just came out about these soldiers who have been frozen for centuries and then thawed out to save the world from destruction with their incredible fighting techniques. Will you take me?"

"What's it rated?"

"Well, I think they gave it an R, but everybody knows they just do that to draw a bigger crowd. The guys at school say it isn't really all that bad. And it's got great special effects."

"No, Zach," I said. "We can't go. It's rated R."

"So? You've taken me to R movies before."

"I shouldn't have."

"But, don't you remember? You said if it was offensive, we'd walk out. And we didn't."

Oh yeah. The big compromise.

Well, this time I held strong. We didn't go to the movie. Zach made no secret of his disgust. He stayed alone in his room, played his music too loud, wasn't interested in going to practice driving. He wasn't interested in me, period. But he got over it.

Six months passed.

"Dad," Russell said. "Guess what's on television?"

It was the movie I'd taken Zach to see. I guess he was right, just about anything you *can* see at the movies you can see on television.

"We are not going to watch that," I told Russell. "It was rated R, and I should never have taken Zach."

He begged. He pleaded. He cleaned his room. He set the table without being asked. He ate his cabbage.

"All right," I said. "We'll compromise. We'll watch it. But, when I say 'Zap!' that means push the remote button and switch channels real fast because there's something coming that I don't want you to see."

The movie was just as thrilling the second time around. So thrilling, in fact, that I got a little overinvolved and forgot to say "Zap!" so Russell and Donovan and Patrick were all treated to the scenes where the man gets impaled and the boy gets terrorized.

Lisa said little before we went to bed. Patrick had a nightmare. And I couldn't sleep either. Guilt. Why in the world, I asked myself, would I let my children watch a movie that worldly people rated R? These were people who might not even have been Christians, and they had decided no one under seventeen should see the movie. Yet I, a Christian father entrusted with these children to show them the way to live, was allowing them to see it.

In the weeks that followed, I was a television tyrant. I discovered sex and violence all over the tube. Overcompensating for my own bad decision, I had pretty much pared down their viewing schedule to reruns of *Leave It to Beaver*. Our science fiction intake was pretty much limited to *My Favorite Martian*. And once, when an underwear commercial came on, my reactions kicked in automatically and I yelled, "Zap!" Terrified, Donovan dropped the remote and covered his head with a pillow.

A few days later I was on my way to a meeting. I was listening to a radio talk-show discussion centered on children of the nineties. The guest speaker—a self-professed authority on children—maintained that parents of the nineties, in order to avoid isolating their children, would have to "embrace reality." His premise was that today's children are different from those of the past, more aware of their rights, more conscious of their choices, more open to change, more able to absorb reality. He warned us—we thousands of out-of-step parents who aren't allowing our children full exposure to the world around them—that we face heartbreak, rebellion, and most likely, loneliness.

And then he said it. "Parents today must be more willing than ever to compromise."

The talk-show host took calls. A lady from New York called in with what she thought was a wonderful example of the benefit of compromise. Her son, "a wholesome all-American type," told his parents he had been having a physical relationship with his girlfriend. The mother, while admitting to initial shock, then reasoned that his confession represented great maturity on his part. In her estimation, her son and this girl would likely continue to "do what comes natural for teenagers" somewhere else. Like in the back of his car. And that would be dangerous.

So she offered a compromise. She would allow them to continue the relationship if they would just do it in his room, where it was safe and clean and comfortable. She sounded so pleased with herself. If she hadn't compromised, she said, she might have lost him.

I felt sick.

That evening at dinner, I looked over my spaghetti fork at the chattering faces crowded around the table. Donovan was trying to tell a joke. He wandered through the story, painfully creeping toward the punch line and, just as he was about to get there, Russell ran out of patience and shouted it out for him. A lesser man would have punched his lights out, but Donovan just slurped his spaghetti.

"I couldn't remember the ending anyway," he shrugged.

The phone rang and Zach went to answer it. Above the roar of the crowd at the table, I overheard part of his conversation.

"Naw," he said. "I can't go. My Dad won't let me see movies that are rated R."

A moment of silence.

"Naw," he said. "He'd find out. Besides, I probably shouldn't see it anyway."

Zach returned to the table and joined in the laughter, once laughing so hard that water went up his nose, grossing out his sister, who used it as an excuse to refuse to eat her English peas.

Donovan tried another joke. Russell ruined it. Lauren finally ate her peas in hopes of angelfood cake. I sat quietly amid the chaos and filed away snapshots in my memory.

"Besides," Zach had said, "I probably shouldn't see it anyway."

Lisa was right. Our children need boundaries. Boundaries to push against. Our children need limits. Limits to define themselves by. They need no. And when we say no, that doesn't mean we'll lose them. It means we love them.

Only one other time has Zach confronted me with the R thing. It was Halloween. He wanted to go see a horror film with a friend. He was testing his limits, pushing against his boundaries. Daring me to stand fast. I accepted the dare. I said no.

"Couldn't we at least compromise?" he asked.

If I wouldn't let him go see that one, would I at least let him rent one? An R-rated one? That way, he said, he'd be watching it at home instead of in a dark theater somewhere.

I thought, Where it's safe and clean? Like the lady on the radio had said?

"No," I said.

"Okay," he said. "That's what I thought."

I think that's what he hoped. Deep inside, I know Zach wanted me to stand fast. It's not easy to do that when the world says to do differently. But we're not of this world. It's not easy to defeat the spirit of compromise. But the Spirit will help us.

It's not easy. But our children are worth it.

12

The Boy Who Rests in the Doorways

A parent away from home, away from his children, thrives on the memories of the unspectacular moments, the day-to-day, what some refer to as the "dull sameness" that is a part of being a family. The moments that mold, the times that tie, those repetitive minutes that knit the father or the mother to the child . . . forever. These are the things we hold on to when we can't hold on to our children.

It is these same moments our children hold on to when they feel insecure and we aren't there to anchor them against the pull of the waves or secure them against the winds that whip around them.

Like us, when they are lonely or sad, it is not the highlights of childhood—the birthday parties, the more expensive gifts, the vacations—they ponder on. It is the softer glow of family life—bedtime stories, roasting marshmallows in the fireplace, kicking a ball just before twilight as the mosquitoes come out, joking around the dinner table, waking up on a cold morning to the sounds of dishes rattling downstairs in the kitchen. These are the things that will warm them when life seems grayer and colder than we prepared them for.

When their hands reach out to find us absent, their minds will search and find us in their hearts.

I took a walk one night in a warm city in the nation of Honduras, far away from my children, but close to them just the same. I knew exactly what they were doing at 10:00 p.m.: sleeping, dreaming perhaps of adventures to be found in the softly falling Oklahoma snow. In my mind's eye, I could hear them sniffling, perhaps from a cold, mumbling in response to a dreamed question, turning beneath a pile of covers, calling out for a drink. Far away we were, but together for sure. For my mind could find them easily in my heart.

Around me milled the people of Honduras, selling oranges, tortillas, mangoes, breads, and pastries, listening to music, telling stories, making friends. The end of a long week, the beginning of a festive weekend. While I was there to observe agricultural projects, I was drawn to the city's streets as strongly as to the farmers' fields.

And then I turned the corner, leaving the fiesta behind, walking out of the sparkling lights into the brooding darkness of the side streets where there was no music or laughter, no oranges or tortillas, no one telling stories, and no one making friends. It was the street of the silent people. A street where even the children don't bother to cry anymore.

I stopped and started to turn away, to return to the more bearable and acceptable crowded city square, when I looked down at my feet and saw the child, as silent and immobile as a sack of potatoes, which he resembled, dressed in dirty burlap, the coarse cloth pulled down and tucked under his feet, pulled up close around his ears. Only his soft, curly dark brown hair showed above the shirt, with the exception of one ear—the left one—which poked out, perhaps to warn him of any danger approaching on the dark streets of Tegulcigalpa.

His knees drawn to his chest, his head resting on his

knees, the boy slept beneath a window on a cobblestone side-walk in the city in which his mother bore him and his father abandoned him.

As I nearly stumbled over him, I thought of my own children, tucked away in their beds with a nightlight—not the moonlight—with blankets, not a burlap bag, to guard against the night. The curls could have been blond, the skin a lighter shade, the eyes blue.

Just a four-year-old boy, sighing on the silent streets, drowsing in the dark doorway, totally devoid of the moments and memories that mold the father to the son, he lay at my feet, totally vulnerable.

More stunning than the sight was the silence. Four-year-old boys are not meant to be so silent, even in sleep. I listened for a sigh and heard only my own. He heard it too, and peeked out through the stretched collar of his shirt, studied my shoes, and slowly angled his head to take me in, almost inch-by-inch, finally making eye contact, only to poke his head deeper into his shell, asleep again.

I walked back around the block and returned to the sparkling lights of the square where the noise reigned, but my heart remained in the darkness of a doorway beneath the muted stars, waiting for a sigh, wishing for a smile, craving for the touch of a tiny hand, aching for a giggle.

I bought an orange and returned to the dark street, but the little one had moved on in search of another doorway, free from the bonds that little boys pull against to grow, full of a hated freedom, craving for a boundary and finding only more room to wander.

In my room that night, I remembered another little boy I met about a decade earlier in another hemisphere. His name was Bivash, and he lived in the city of Faridpur in Bangladesh. A sophomore in college, I had gone there for the summer to work as a missionary, teaching college students English and working—playing—with the children who surrounded the mission compound.

Bivash was a source of great joy for me, for he had the grandest smile I had ever seen. His round, brown eyes looked as if they would explode, they grew so large and sparkled so brightly before he would burst into a laughter that made his feet leave the floor and his hands wave wildly above his head. Once I got used to the fact that Bivash would laugh anytime I came into sight, I enjoyed his presence and welcomed him as he followed me around the mission grounds.

I had stumbled on him just as I had the Honduran. Standing on the veranda of the mission office, I was watching what appeared to be a large, brown bird popping up and down in the middle of the sea of bright, green grass that spread for acres in front of the building. I stood alone, watching this bird bend and snatch bugs from the grass. I longed to see it take flight.

And then it stood and walked toward me. Not a bird, but a boy, carrying a small pair of scissors with which he had been trimming the taller pieces of grass that marred the carpet-like landscape. Instead of a big bird, it was a very small boy.

The eighth son of a rickshaw driver, Bivash had been sent into the city to earn his way. He could either beg or become gainfully employed, which he had done, persuading the mission groundskeeper to pay him the equivalent of a few pennies a day to trim weeds with his very valuable scissors.

Bivash, the groundskeeper told me, had great dreams. He planned to go to school someday, then to college in the United States, then to return as an engineer to build dams and bridges to protect his family from the never-ending floods and typhoons that invaded his country.

In the meantime, Bivash's main goal in life was to chatter away in his native tongue and laugh. And laughter was a language I could understand. A giggle from Bivash erased the loneliness that always greeted me in the morning when I looked out on the coconut trees and rice paddies and saw the gathering clouds preparing for the afternoon monsoon rains. This wasn't Texas in the summertime.

My summer in Bangladesh ended with days of torrential rain and devastating floods that swept through Faridpur, knocking homes off foundations, adding thousands to the city's poor, sending the homeless running for unavailable shelter. I could see rickshaws floating down the street, taking men's livelihoods with them to the Ganges River, swollen and rampaging, wrecking fishermen's boats. The huge lawn of the mission became a lake, and we evacuated while the roads were still open.

I never saw Bivash again. I'll never see the boy in the doorway again. What is important is what they taught me. I do not have to hunger to want to feed the hungry. I do not have to sleep in a doorway to want to shelter the homeless. I do not have to wear burlap to seek to clothe the naked. I do not have to be ignorant to understand the desire for education. I do not have to be hopeless to understand hope. I do not have to be without to understand the need to give.

Somewhere there is a young man in Central America whom I pray no longer wanders; somewhere in Bangladesh a young man I pray is studying to be an engineer. Just a couple of small voices that spoke to my heart.

Oh, how I pray that someone will do for my children what these boys did for me. That someone will open their eyes. That someone will speak to their hearts, teach them to be compassionate, to love the unlovely, to give and to teach. Oh sure, I can tell them. I can encourage them. But sometimes it takes turning away from the festivities of the familiar and walking into a dark alley. And listening.

13

A Slip of the Tongue

Russell was having a bad-hair day. Which means we were all having a bad-hair day. No matter how hard he tried, no matter how much hairspray he pumped into the atmosphere, he could not achieve that perfect, every-strand-in-place summer-blond trademark do of his.

I used to be more patient with such tragedies, but it's becoming harder and harder to relate directly. His hair is there. What more could he want?

"This is the cruddiest hairspray ever invented, and naturally, we buy the biggest size they sell," he yelled, emerging from the bathroom with a towel over his head. He tossed the container into the dirty-clothes hamper as he came through the door.

"I'm not going to handbell practice. I'm not going to choir. I'm not going to church. And no, I'm not going to shut up!"

His cheeks were flushed, his eyes were watering, and his hair was hilarious. So, what did I do? Put my arms around him and offer my sincerest sympathy for his hairy predicament? Lend him an industrial strength wire brush to remove the dozen coats of spray? Yank the mirror from the wall to alleviate his pain and suffering and begin the slow process of rebuilding his self-esteem? Lecture him gently on the ruinous effect of vanity on a sparkling personality? None of the above?

Right. I laughed.

He pulled the towel over his face, began to moan seriously, and somehow stumbled up the stairs to his bedroom where he vowed loudly never to see me again, making it clear that every other boy in the world had a more understanding dad than he did. With better hair.

Why is it that when I am on a roll, when things are going so well, when I'm really humming and doing so marvelously well at this daddy thing, I just fall all over myself to reveal my callous side? Why is it this cruel human side emerges every time I think I'm perfecting my performance?

Zach came down the stairs.

"Russell just growled at me from under a towel," he said. "What's eatin' him?"

Ah . . . fresh game.

"Zach?" I asked. "Not to be picky or anything, but do you remember that I took you driving in the cemetery a couple of days ago . . . because you asked? And, Zach, do you remember that you said if I would take you driving, you would clean out my car and wash it? And, Zach, do you realize it's been absolutely beautiful outside and my car's still a mess? Two days after the fact."

A vacant stare. Oh yes, that always warms the father's heart.

"And, Zach, do you remember asking me yesterday afternoon if you could move the car out of the way so you could play basketball? That pretty well shoots any excuse about there not being enough time to get the car clean. Doesn't it?"

A few mumbles began to take form as he prepared his defense. Well, I was having none of that.

"I won't put up with laziness . . . or your making promises just to get your way around here. Understand?"

Whatever he had come downstairs for, it must not have been too important because he turned around and went right back up without saying a word. Now why doesn't he just learn to express himself? I was right there.

"Daddy?" Lauren called from her bedroom. "I need you."

"I'm busy," I barked. "Is it really important?"

No answer. I guess it wasn't.

I looked around to see if anyone else was in the mood to talk. Seeing no one, I went into the bathroom to shave and discovered the incredible mess Russell had left behind to remind us of his cowlick catastrophe.

"Russell!" I yelled. "You get down here this instant and clean up this mess. What do you want me to do with you? Send you to the Boys Ranch?"

The very walls gasped. The wattage in the light fixtures dropped as a gloom descended over the once-happy home. Lauren ceased her chattering. Lisa wasn't humming. Zachary poked his head out his door. Donovan and Patrick ended their own argument in mid-sentence. Even the dog dropped her bone. I could see tomorrow's headlines on the daily paper: "How *Could* You?"

All ears were on the moaning upstairs, which shifted immediately from its exhaustive chant to a hysterical wail, much like a tornado-warning siren.

Hey, it was just a slip of the tongue.

"I'll apologize," I told the finger-pointing world. "He knows I didn't mean it."

"But he knows you thought it," said Lisa, the only one who still thought I was at least worthy of recognition as a still-functioning organism. A very lowly specimen, no doubt, but still here. Very uncomfortably so.

"I think I'll go straighten up the bathroom," I mumbled, and since no one urgently seemed to need me near, I slunk out.

In the days that followed, I took advantage of every opportunity I could find or manufacture to convince Russell that I loved him. And every attempt was met with deserved skepticism.

I tried to explain myself. But there *was* no explanation. On top of flattening my tender offspring with a taste of rejection, I had referred to the ministry of the Boys Ranch in a negative way, as if it were a place of punishment rather than a place of promise. And I know firsthand, having been a Boys Ranch houseparent myself, that many of the boys who spend part of their lives there do so because their parents have problems, not them.

I tried to explain that to Russell, and to his credit, he controlled his own tongue. He had every right to say, "Well then, maybe I *should* go there, because you've definitely got problems."

Russell stayed mad longer than I thought he was capable of. I was accustomed to his up-and-down swings, so I had consoled myself, saying my accidental insults probably rolled off Russell like water off a duck's back. Now I know they don't. Not when they come from Dad. My slip of the tongue was delivered with the force of a sledgehammer.

"Russell?" I was sitting on the edge of his bed, untangling a knot in his numchucks string. "Do you know how much I love you?"

A long pause.

"Yes," he said. "I think you love me very much."

I was overwhelmed. I didn't even have to tell him how miserable I'd been. I cleared my throat and wiped back tears with the sleeve of my shirt. I had prepared for the worst. He could have said, "Oh sure, Dad. That's why you want to send me away." But he didn't say that, because he knows I wouldn't do it. Not for a messy bathroom. Not for the world.

My confidence level zoomed as I turned out his light and headed downstairs. My almost exemplary, long-term parenting skills had saved me again, allowing me to survive one thoughtless error. Surely I could be forgiven such a minor slip of the tongue.

Lisa caught me at the bottom of the stairs, totally exasperated.

"I give up," she said. "I think you better go have a talk with your number-one son."

Zach? What could possibly be wrong with Zach?

I sprinted back upstairs with a confident spring in my step. Hey, Russell loved me again. I was on a roll.

To nowhere.

Turns out Zach had been hurt just as much as Russell and, not only that, but the hurt had been compounded by all the attention I'd paid to Russell the past few days. Zachary's a teenager. Teenage boys don't cry and kick the wall. They hole up and listen to the radio. And everybody thinks they're just being teenagers.

Did I really think he was lazy? Did I really think he made promises just to get his own way?

"No, Zach. Of course not."

"Well, that's what you said."

"Hey, it was just a . . . a slip of the tongue."

And then he flung his fury back at me with full force.

"So what are you going to do now, Dad?" he said, looking me straight in the eyes. "Send me to the Boys Ranch?"

I felt small enough to search for a hiding place among the carpet fibers. When I finally slunk back down the stairs about an hour later, all the confidence I had paraded in regarding my parenting skills had drained from me. I wasn't sure if Zach forgave me because I blubbered around till he was on the verge of exhaustion, or if he really meant it. Time, and his penchant for honest expression of emotions, would tell.

I thought back to how this mess began. Russell and his bad-hair day. *He* was having the bad day, not me. So I guess the first thing I cheated myself out of was a chance to be a comforter.

Then there was Zach, just trotting down the stairs with a smile on his face and a question in his eyes. I guess I'll never know what he was thinking or what he was wanting. Instead, I took him, a teenager with the typical self-doubts of people his age, and brought him down another notch or two. So I guess the second thing I cheated myself out of was the chance to be an encourager.

Then there was Lauren, sitting quietly around the corner in her own little room, an innocent victim of my lack of control. "Daddy?" she'd said. "I need you." "I'm busy," I'd barked. "Is it really important?" Maybe it was. I guess I cheated myself out of being needed.

I went from Zachary's room into her room where she was sleeping, her knees pulled up under her chin, her soft stuffed rabbit sharing her pillow. And I sat there awhile. Just in case she needed me.

We all say things we shouldn't say. And we hurt people we love. And sometimes when we do, we just say, "Tough, that's just the way I am. Learn to live with it."

Unfortunately, our children usually do just that. They let us get away with it. They just blow it off and unwittingly create an invisible gap, a difficult distance between us. They build a little barrier to protect themselves against the next unpredictable slip. And if we don't pay close attention to the signals they're sending, we think they're doing just fine. So when they seek comfort, or encouragement, or just need us, we're having a bad-mouth day.

It's a dangerous thing, that slip of the tongue.

14

You and Me and the Deep Blue Sea

"Don't you feel just a tad guilty?" I asked Lisa, as her parents drove out of sight with all five children.

"Nope," she said.

"Me neither," I said. "They're getting exactly what they asked for, five little angels. In a week, they can send the little devils home."

That settled, we went inside to finish packing our own suitcases for our first trip alone together in years. The house seemed to sigh as we entered. I don't know, maybe it felt guilty. The rooms were silent. The television was off. There was no music. No arguing. It was dull, and fascinating, almost like I'd never been there before. We'd gone from chaos to calm so fast I told Lisa I wasn't sure I could adjust.

"I'll help you," she smiled slyly. "It'll be fun."

Sounded promising to me.

Within an hour we were headed south on the interstate. Within three hours we were in Texas. Within ten hours we were in a whole new world. We'd gone from the windy land-locked plains to the sandy ocean beach in hardly longer than it takes to fold a day's worth of laundry.

We had a condo for a week, courtesy of Lisa's generous aunt and uncle.

"We raised five children too," they explained to Lisa when she collapsed into a blubbering mass of gratitude on the telephone. "We understand."

Frankly, the idea was kind of spooky. We hadn't really been alone together in a long time. In fact, the last time we'd gotten away together had been at a marriage retreat, and we'd ended up sitting up half the night talking with another couple about child-rearing problems they were having. We had other things on our minds, before we got too tired.

I know that to be a good parent, you really have to have a whole lot more in your life than just your kids. If your whole life is wrapped up in your kids, then when they leave home someday, you're just a bunch of wrapping paper around a big, empty box.

From the very moment I agreed to take the time off from work, let the children pack off to their grandparents', and hit the road with her, Lisa had been downright giddy. She sat at the dining table and pored over brochures describing the condominium, the restaurants, the beaches, the theaters, the historical sites, and the museums. She wrote up little menus for the meals we'd share, sitting on the patio of the condo, listening to the surf.

She started packing the essentials two weeks early—lots of candles, scented body oils, and new lingerie. What, no coloring books?

"You need to quit looking so anxious," I told her one evening. "You're gonna make the kids unstable. Somebody will probably start wetting the bed."

But all that was behind us now, and we were in the lap of luxury with lots of time, a minimum amount of cash, and an alarming amount of solitude.

"So, what now?" I asked.

"What a romantic," she replied.

"No, really," I said. "What do you want to do first? Your wish is my command. Within reason."

All the practicality of motherhood obviously doesn't melt away in one ten-hour drive. She suggested we buy groceries first, so we ignored the call of the waves and headed down the asphalt to peruse the aisles of goodies to fill those scrumptious menus she'd prepared so diligently.

"Now," she cautioned. "Don't run. And don't beg."

I just kind of stopped and stared at her for a second, and she came around pretty quickly.

"Oops," she said. "I'm used to shopping with Donovan and Patrick. They like to open the cereal boxes to look for surprises. But do be careful, dear, especially in the syrup aisle. Those bottles would as soon tumble off on to the floor as look at you. Believe me, I know."

"Yes, Mommy," I said.

Back at the condo, we changed into something more comfortable—shorts—and promised we wouldn't make fun of each other. Lying was allowed.

While Lisa cooked dinner, I sat out on the patio and watched dolphins play in the waves. Fishing boats, swarmed by seagulls, moved back and forth on the sea, bringing in the goodies for all the restaurants we were planning to hit on our trip.

"Donovan would love those fishing boats," I said. "And Lauren would have a fit over those dolphins. Can you imagine how excited Zachary will be to see those waves? I can't wait to see Patrick chase those crabs on the beach. You think Russell will get a kick out of building sand castles? I mean, they haven't been to Galveston since Patrick was a baby. Lauren wasn't even born then."

That earlier trip had provided good memories. Galveston in October. Despite the cool temperatures, we'd been enticed into the water in our clothes. I was holding Patrick by his tiny little hands, his just-as-tiny little feet dangling in the waves. Then, when Zachary distracted me to look his way at a shell he'd found, a huge wave drenched Patrick head to toe.

"Sweetie," Lisa said, "you're rambling. And you've broken rule number one."

Oh yeah, rule number one. That was my idea. We weren't going to talk about the kids for at least twenty-four hours. This was our trip.

"Have you by chance seen anything I might like?" she asked hopefully. "After all, I'm here and they aren't."

"Nope," I kidded. "I didn't see a thing you'd like. Guess you'll have to be satisfied with me."

"No problem," she said.

Slowly but surely we got used to just being with each other again. I had forgotten how comfortable she could be when no one is needing a homework paper checked, a permission slip signed, a Band-Aid applied, hair braided, a glass of water. I had forgotten how calm she could be when there are no arguments to settle, birthday parties to plan, or teacher conferences to attend. I had forgotten that once upon a time, there was just her and me. And I had definitely forgotten how nice that can be.

Oh sure, there were slip-ups, like when we went to the fanciest seafood restaurant on the coast and automatically turned to the children's menu. There was one little argument, sparked by her refusal to let me go into the souvenir shops until the children arrived later in the week. And when we sat on the beach, we just naturally had a tendency to spot kids that looked like ours. Then we'd grow quiet for a few seconds. But it was temporary.

We visited antique shops, toured old mansions, drove the length of the island just to see how easy it is when it's just the two of us. We had double-dip ice cream cones on a romantic gray day on our way back from our third ferry ride.

And we spent our evenings "getting in touch" with each other, thankful that God is so creative and imaginative. It was during these tender times that we realized that having had to stretch and modify and share our love with five others during our sixteen years together had not strained it, reduced it, or weakened it. If anything, it was much stronger, for it carried with it now the comfort of familiarity, the fuller understanding of our needs and the selflessness of our oneness.

Only once or twice in the years we have been married has my mind wandered far enough into the future to envision a time beyond our children, a time when they are busy with their own young families, devoting their time to wives and a husband and our . . . grandchildren. At that point, my wandering usually shifted quickly into reverse. But, I had always been a little concerned about what we would do with our time when our children are not here to fight each other for it.

That week in Galveston assured me. My time will be spent with the lady I love. The woman God gave me. Yes, the mother of my children, but only because I married her first and loved her faithfully.

"It's still there," she said, speaking of our love.

"Were you worried?" I asked.

"Well, not really," she said. "Although I was a bit concerned it had gotten buried in a pile of ironing somewhere, never to be found."

"That happens to shirts," I said. "Not love."

"Promise?"

"Cross my heart and hope to die."

"Stick a thousand needles in your eye?"

Apparently, we were beginning to miss the children again, which was pretty good timing, since they were to arrive in the morning after spending a week with grandparents who do everything from taking them up in hang gliders and feeding them steaks all week to indulging them with round after round of board games. I wondered if a week was long enough to spoil somebody.

I decided it was, for I realized I was spoiled. Away from the demands of motherhood, Lisa had concentrated on my needs, listened to my dreams, concentrated on my concerns, put a Band-Aid on my hurts. I may not have a small voice, but I do need attention.

The night before our family came back together, my bride and I sat on the seawall, and in the moonlight we pledged our love anew. We did it for ourselves and we did it for our children, for there is nothing more valuable we can give to them than to love each other as much as we love them.

We were reunited with Zachary, Russell, Donovan, Patrick, and Lauren in Aunt Maurine's living room. They presented us with gifts: pictures they had drawn, souvenirs from San Antonio's Sea World, a nature scene of treasures plucked from the trail behind their grandparents' home.

"You look happy," Russell said innocently, looking me in the eyes with a puzzled expression on his face.

"Thank you," I said simply. And then I looked at my wife.

"Thank you," I said simply.

15

And Don't Forget
Babies-to-Be

"Don't forget babies-to-be."

Donovan said it again. It had become number one on the prayer-request hot line. My search for just the right time to broach this subject had come to an end. Something this firmly placed on his heart was begging for attention.

"Donnie?" I asked. "Before we pray, would you like to talk about these babies-to-be that you're so concerned about?"

"Well," he said, "I just don't get it. I've been thinking about it awhile and I just don't get it."

When Donovan chooses something to think about, he tends to do it for a while, examining all the angles, collecting the evidence, listening to the arguments and then, he usually brightens and exclaims, "Oh! I get it!"

Then he comes out of his mysterious cloud and plays until something else comes along that demands all his intellectual energy.

I looked at my son, only eleven, yet confronting and

107

trying to reason out a concept he has found intolerable. He has heard something somewhere about abortion, and he wants his daddy to tell him what he heard was not true. Where is the innocence we expect from big-eared little boys who can one moment put on a cape and leap about saving civilization as a superhero, and then drop the cape and, puzzled, ask about abortion?

"What is it you don't get?" I asked.

"Okay," he said. "It's like this. All of us were babies once, right?"

"Right."

"Okay," he said. "But some babies get aborted. I don't get what happens to them."

"Well," I said. "They just never get born. To people it's like they never existed."

"I don't get it," he said. "If, like you told me, God already knew me way back when I was still inside Mom, then wouldn't God want me to be born?"

"Yes, Donnie," I said. "God would."

"And didn't you say that God knows all about my life even before I'm born?"

"Yes, Donnie. I said that."

"But," he said, "if Mom had decided she didn't want me to be born, she could have gotten rid of me even though God wanted me to be born? Even though He had things He wanted me to do?"

"That's right," I said. "She could have, but she wouldn't have."

"But some moms do," he said, scratching his head. "I don't get it."

"I don't think God gets it either," I said. "I think Heaven weeps."

"Why do mommies do it? Get abortions?" he asked.

I thought hard for a moment. It was a good question, and there were lots of ways it could be answered, depending on one's political views, but it really came down to one word.

"Convenience," I answered. "To them, it just seems like the best way out of a situation they wish they weren't in."

He was quiet. Reflective. Pensive.

"You mean," he said, "if Mommy had gotten pregnant with me at a time when it wouldn't be 'convenient' to have me, she could have killed me? I would never have been born? Because it was too much trouble?"

It sounded especially brutal coming from the mouth of a child. I assured him that convenience was never a word that had much meaning to his mother.

"Donnie," I said. "Once, when you were just three days old, I woke up and saw Mom holding you in the middle of the night. Those few precious moments alone make up to her for all the inconvenience you'll ever bring to her life."

Waking up in the middle of the night to see her with her children had been a satisfying habit of mine.

"My Sunday school teacher says abortion is murder," said Donovan. "When I watch television and somebody murders somebody, they go to jail. Do people who get abortions go to jail?"

I explained to Donovan that abortions are legal and that, while they do end a life, the world we live in doesn't consider it murder.

"I know," I said. "You don't get it. Neither do I, but remember this, Donovan: We are not of this world."

Donovan shared with me a secret fear he'd had that his mother would get put in jail and be on the nightly news. For weeks, as she took Russell to his baseball practices, they had passed an abortion clinic where protestors were marching. Lisa would honk and wave her support. One night, Donovan wasn't with her when she took Russell to his practice. Instead, Donovan was home watching the news and they showed abortion protestors being arrested and taken off to jail.

"I thought they got Mom," he said. "For being against abortions."

I tried to explain that, because of the laws, a woman could kill a baby and not be arrested, but a protestor, if she went on private property without permission, could be. He was bewildered. "It goes on every day, doesn't it, Dad?" he asked sadly. "Aborting babies."

My heart broke. I remembered the times his fish would die, or his hamster, or a kitten, or even a squirrel in the street. Tenderly, Donovan would carry the lifeless body to the back yard, dig a little hole, place it inside, cover it, and place a cross and flowers on the grave. For a while, Donovan would be quieter than usual, then he would go on his merry way.

He had a tender heart. We'd had a long talk one time after his first hamster died. He was younger then and had even more questions. Finally, I convinced him that he would not have to live his life wondering if the hamster would be waiting in Heaven.

"Hamsters have no soul," I explained.

"Babies do," he had said. Who knows? Maybe even then he was concerned about babies-to-be and the burgeoning nursery full of little souls in Heaven.

But now, he was eleven and he'd heard plenty about abortion, from the marches on television to the honest convictions of a Sunday school teacher.

"Why do we let them do it?" he asked. "Why don't we just let people who love babies have the ones other people don't want? That's what I would do."

I explained that a lot of people just don't believe that a baby is a baby until it's born. These people put themselves in God's place and, even though He said He knows us in the womb, they don't believe Him.

"I guess they just don't know Him," he said.

We talked on for a while. I told him how thankful I was that I had fallen in love with a woman who understands the sanctity of life, who believes in a loving God, who knows that every heart is precious to Jesus and that He mourns when one stops beating. Every child deserves a chance to explore the life God so carefully constructed for him.

"What brought all this on?" I asked.

"I was lying in bed the other night and I heard Lauren telling Mom about something that happened at school. She was crying, and she said something about how nobody liked her. I like her."

I was trying to follow his logic. He went on.

"Well, anyway," he said. "I was thinking about what a pain she is sometimes, and I went on thinking about what a pain all my brothers are. But I like them all."

"Okay," I said.

"Mom could have aborted them, couldn't she?" he asked. "She could have killed them and never been punished for it. And I would never even have known it. Or them.

"She could have aborted me."

Donnie had put his finger on the real reason abortion is unacceptable to God. It violates God's law that governs everything: love.

For God so loved the world that He gave His only begotten Son so we could . . . what? Kill our children? I think not. He loved and gave so we could live. Life has never been a frivolous thing to God.

When I turned out the light, I pondered the question about punishment. Surrounded by the soft, steady breathing of my children, I realized that not having them would be the punishment. They are gifts from God, not to be taken lightly. I should think it is an awesome mistake to refuse a gift from God.

God bless the babies-to-be.

16

The Worst Thing That Ever Happened

Once upon a time there was a child who lived in a small town where little boys and girls went barefoot, chased horny toads, fished for crawdads, wrestled with dogs on the cool, green grass, and sold lemonade down on the corner.

This child, this little boy, always wore blue jeans and striped T-shirts and black high-top tennis shoes. He was a basically happy child. He cried, but no more often than most little boys. When he was angry, he was easily distracted, for he was very interested in the world around him. He never curled up in frustration or pulled the covers over his head in shadowy loneliness. He never brushed away tears with the back of his hand or buried a sad face in the softness of his dog. Life was not perfect, but he *was* a happy child.

This child never woke at night and wondered why. He never had a knot in his stomach as big as an apple. He never stared out the window without seeing. But that was once upon a time. That was "before."

I am often reminded of "before" when I see my children

heading down the street on roller blades or out back to the creek with a rod and reel. Or laughing upstairs after the lights go out. Not that they don't sometimes cry . . . or get angry . . . or hurt. All of those things are the instruments of change that, combined with the moments of victory, success, and acceptance, make them who they are.

Zachary and I had just left the basketball game, and he was recalling the unfortunate way in which his team almost lost the game. They were ahead by one point with two seconds left, and Zachary committed the foul that sent the player to the line to shoot one and one. The boy made the first and missed the second, sending the game into overtime and a very dejected and embarrassed Zachary to the bench. He wasn't exactly high-fived on arrival. Fortunately, his team won.

"That's about the worst thing that's ever happened to me," he said in the car. "If we'd lost that game, I'd have never forgotten it."

Then Zachary asked me what was the worst thing that had ever happened to me as a kid. I knew where he was coming from. Had I ever split my pants in English class? Had a pimple the size of Mount Rushmore on the end of my nose? Struck out to end the ninth inning of a losing game? Wet the bed while spending the night with a friend? I started to tell him about the worst thing that ever happened to me, but I froze up. It was too beautiful a day. I told him something else, something trivial in comparison to the truth.

"I think," I said, "that the worst thing that ever happened to me was when I asked Joanie Parker to go to my high school homecoming with me in the tenth grade. She'd been dating seniors, but for some reason, she didn't have a date. So I asked, and she said yes."

"So," said Zach. "What was so bad about that?"

In my book, Joanie was the most gorgeous girl in school. She had long, honey-colored hair, a great laugh, and really pretty eyes. My stature among the sophomore guys skyrocketed.

"I borrowed my stepbrother's Mustang convertible," I remembered. "And I picked her up an hour before the game. She was in her drill-team uniform so she could perform with the other high-steppers at half time. She had great legs."

After the game, Joanie changed clothes, pinned on her homecoming mum, and we headed to the dance.

I was in love. And so was Joanie.

Within an hour she was disappearing frequently to the ladies room. Then she asked me if I would please take her home because she had a terrible headache. So I moped out to the freezing parking lot, warmed up my stepbrother's Mustang, and picked her up at the gymnasium door. She was smiling and laughing with her girlfriends and looked okay to me, but swore that her head was splitting and she just didn't want to let everyone know. She didn't want to spoil anyone else's fun.

On her porch, she apologized that she couldn't let me kiss her goodnight. "I could be contagious."

I was still in love. And so was Joanie. But not with me.

Just driving on her street gave me a thrill, just staring at the porch on which I stood with her made my heart pound, so I drove around the block a couple of times.

On about the fourth time around, I saw Joanie Parker and Gary Landham, a senior on the football team, stepping off her porch. He had his arm around her. She was laughing again. There was no pained expression on her face. They got in his car and left. And they never saw me.

"And that's about the worst thing that ever happened to me," I said to Zach.

"Whoa," he said. "Cruel thing."

Yes, I said to myself. Rejection is a cruel thing. But it isn't really the worst thing that ever happened to me. Not by any stretch. By comparison, it's just a bittersweet memory.

There are some memories that never become bitter-sweet. Such as my memory of the incident that fills that dark era between "before" and "after."

I was a little boy. My parents had been divorced almost a year, and there was still an aching emptiness I was sure would never go away. Everything was a reminder. The space in the driveway where Daddy used to park his car. The absence of ashtrays in the living room. No Vienna sausages in the cabinet. No snoring at night. No weekend fishing trips.

Mother soon decided, rightly so, that my brother Mike and I needed to be around males, not cooped up all the time in a house with a mother and two sisters. So, we joined a bunch of guys who were trying to start up a Scouting troop under a Mr. Wailey, a young, clean-cut outdoorsman who was new to Denton. Mr. Wailey was not a Scout leader, but he promised he'd run his troop just like a real one.

We took to him right off. He reminded me of all the good things I remembered about Daddy. Mr. Wailey even decided I could hang around with the troop, even though I wasn't really old enough, being only eight. Mr. Wailey assured my mom he'd take me under his wing and protect me from the older boys. I'd get "special attention."

Mr. Wailey was a pedophile. And I was a lonely, broken-hearted little boy who'd recently lost his father. I was in deep need of an adult man worthy of my trust and attention. I was ignorant and innocent and eager to be accepted. For six months, Mr. Wailey "protected" me, until a boy with an even younger brother joined the troop. And then I was rejected.

He was a sick man with a twisted mind and a way of making evil look like love. And he took it upon himself to reshape the lives of unwary children. With a false smile and a corrupted touch, he took childhood simplicity and innocence and turned it into premature guilt and confusion. He took the gentle psyche of an innocent boy in his perverted hands and twisted it so hard that he left a permanent imprint on the future shape of my life. And from all of this, he gained his wicked satisfaction.

After he traded me in, I retreated into a shell, custom-built a safer world around me, and became very selective about who could enter.

"He's such a serious child." "A little intellectual." "So timid." "A deep thinker." People thought they had me figured out, but I was so hidden inside myself, they hadn't a clue.

For years I could not touch or be touched. I could not say to anyone, "I love you." I could not believe it when anyone said it to me.

Whose fault was it? For years, I believed it was mine. But I had been only an innocent, unaware, lonely child. Later, I decided it was my mother's fault, for putting me so directly in harm's way, for trusting my needs to a perfect stranger. Yet, she was only acting in my behalf and made a mistake out of ignorance and trust herself. Next, I blamed my brother for not seeing what was going on, for being so naive, for putting the troop before me.

And then I realized it was all Mr. Wailey's fault. But he was gone and I couldn't hurl my hurt back at him.

It was only a brief "relationship," but like all children preyed upon by sick adults, I did not escape undamaged.

But was what Mr. Wailey did to me the worst thing that ever happened to me? Not in itself.

When I was cast aside by Mr. Wailey and able to think more clearly, it didn't take me long to know how wrong it had all been. Feeling real guilt for the first time in my life, I went to a grownup I thought I could trust. He had come to me when my father had gone and told me he "was there for me."

"I've been doing something terrible. Can I tell you about it?" I remember asking.

"Yes," he said. "You can tell me anything."

And I did. And I thought he was listening. And I thought he would help me.

"Don't you ever repeat a word of this to anyone," he said angrily. "People will call you a liar and a lot of other things.

There's no excuse for making things up just to get attention."

In retrospect, I think he was reacting out of his own guilt. Maybe he felt if he'd "been there for me," this would never have happened.

So I went to my brother. He was just a young teenager, but he seemed like a grownup to me.

"Mike," I said. "Mr. Wailey's a bad man."

And I told him the truth. And he hit me in the face. And he called me a liar. It didn't seem to bother him at all that I wouldn't go to troop meetings with him anymore.

Through the years, I have thought about the two people I had gone to for help. Two people I had trusted. Two people who wouldn't listen. Looking back, *that* was the worst thing that ever happened to me.

I never told anyone else for a long time. I had decided grownups just don't listen to small voices.

Years later, after I became a grownup myself, I asked my brother why he reacted as he did. You know what? He didn't even remember the incident. After all, he was just a kid, and he acted just like a kid would act. I know that now.

I don't know what eventually became of Mr. Wailey. I have lain awake at night wondering about the hurt and damage he inflicted on the little boys who followed me. Hurt that might have been prevented if someone had listened to my cry for help. I have prayed through the years that someone would stop him. If I could have found him, that someone would have been me.

A few times, anger and depression have attacked me. Only God's Spirit that fills me can overpower it. That same Spirit continues to clean out my wounds and lessen my scars.

If I had not become a Christian, I cannot imagine what I would be like today. Still in a shell? Still afraid to touch or be touched? Unable to tell my children "I love you"?

Even as a Christian, emerging from the darkness took time. The building of trust was not an easy thing for me. But, before I was a Christian, I had not known true forgiveness.

I had never experienced joy, except briefly. And that was "before."

Only God can use people to rebuild a broken heart. Like a wife who looks deep inside and carefully, patiently unlocks doors rusted shut from lack of use. And like miraculous children who love so naturally and so unselfishly and so fully that one cannot hide from such love. Sometimes I still sit alone at the end of a day and marvel: they love me. And I learned to say "I love you," for I know so well how desperately a child needs to hear it and believe it and take refuge in it.

I never used to tell anyone about the worst thing that ever happened to me until I realized that it still happens to so many innocent children. Children whose parents would give up their own lives to protect them from abuse. But abuse is slick and tricky and well disguised. It slips into a child's world with a smile and a laugh and doesn't leave until childhood purity has been stolen away or destroyed.

I pray for God's protection for my children. I pray that He will give me keen eyes to spot evil and that He will guide my family away from it. And I pray for God's healing for the children who have been lured into darkness and suffer silent shame.

It is a sad world we live in where children get hurt by people they want to trust and love. It is a sad world where a child invites someone in to fill a void and that person fills it with guilt, pain, and tragedy. It is a sad world where a child's plea for help goes unanswered, compounding his puzzlement. It is a sad world when people don't listen when a soul is crying.

That's the worst thing that can happen.

17

Getting My Act Together

What a difference a year makes. From one Christmas to the next, I had fallen from stardom to extra, joining the ranks of other former main characters who are given the roles of street beggars and market merchants. Three lines. Three simple lines.

Actually, I was supposed to be a temple scholar, dignified, serious, and spiritual. But I looked more like a nun. Robes and shawls do nothing for me. My stage presence wasn't exactly enhanced when I forgot to remove my glasses . . . a little modern for the New Testament era, and a little distracting for the guys dressed as wise men with whom this scholar fellow was to converse.

So as it turned out, I would be remembered for wearing my glasses and for the brightness of the lipstick the makeup ladies lavished on me to make sure my three big lines would be noticed.

My big role, during my brief moment in the spotlight, was to mislead the Magi. When they asked me to take them to the "King," I was to do so. But to the wrong king. In all my wisdom and spirituality, I was to lead them to evil. To Herod.

"Come with me," I said, in my loudest, deepest, most expressive stage voice. "I will see if an audience with the king can be arranged." And then I led them to a dead end, a stumbling block on the pathway to eternity. My role was through.

Backstage, waiting for the finale when I would make my final reverential entrance, I thought about how many times people today come out in their royal robes of righteousness and offer to take people to the King and then lead them on a dead-end stroll, stumbling far off the heavenly path.

The big question is, who am I when I take off the robes and the makeup? If children follow the path I take, will it point them in the direction of the King? Not because I'm a Sunday school teacher. Not because I'm a deacon. Not because I am practiced in providing the answers children are supposed to be given.

When I'm not in the classroom or the sanctuary or the business meeting or the council meeting, will I be a road sign? When I don't know someone is watching, will they see Jesus in me?

Am I a guide for children and young people who see me at church and in my home? If God saw someone in need of a guide, would He ask me? Would I respond?

Because God used great men throughout my life, I myself am on the pathway to Heaven, assured to spend an eternity with Jesus. When I look back, I can see occasions where God used men in my life. Men who did not say no. Men who made a difference.

It started when I was young.

"It'll be all right. You'll see."

Mother always said those words as we pulled up behind grocery stores to search for cardboard boxes. Moving again. I always knew it would not be all right.

Ever since my real dad left—during my first-grade year—

we'd been on the road. My stepfather, who said he loved my mother but had little patience for four small children, would lose a job, get drunk, gamble away the rent, and there we were again, clearing out by week's end, just ahead of the landlord. Friends never knew where we disappeared to.

Mother was always taking us to new churches to be influenced by the right kind of people—people who were different from the types who came over on Friday nights to play poker. Summers she'd haul us to vacation Bible schools. Christmas and Easter we'd make the rounds of special programs.

"You need to know these things," she'd say. "There's a better life and I want you to know about it."

And then one day my stepfather left and didn't come back.

"It'll be all right," Mother said, as we crowded into my grandparents' house.

By then, because of a revival at a new church in Houston that my mother had insisted we attend—night after night—I had given my life to Jesus. I was a Christian, but I was so timid in the Spirit that no one would have guessed.

One thing I did do as a Christian was pray, so when my stepfather left, I prayed and prayed and prayed that Mother would meet no more men.

And then she married again.

In my utmost Christian maturity, I disregarded God and prepared for impending doom. At least, I thought, being a junior in high school, I can leave after next year and be on my own.

But love came down. For ten beautiful years, George loved my mother, kept her on a pedestal, celebrated the goodness of a godly woman, dedicated his life to meeting her family's needs, worked hard to erase decades of pain, rebuilt self-worth in bewildered children not even his own, unknowingly taught us all about love and trust.

Life had been composed of the burden of the past and

the fear of the future. Now there was something new. There was the joy of the present.

George died of cancer at the age of fifty-two, and we felt a new kind of separation, a different kind of sorrow, a deeper form of pain. Because of love. Because of this love, we held each other close as a family and gave each other strength. We regarded God and dwelt on Him. He healed our hurts.

This simple man, an aircraft engine mechanic with common sense and a gentle, caring heart, had shown me, without making a show of it, how God's love comes down through the hands and hearts of those who know Him. George was a guide.

A year after George had come into our home, I did leave for college. If anyone had known I was there, they could have voted me the quietest man on campus or the one most likely to fade into oblivion. I was merely a shadow, stunned by the bravado and outspokenness of the other students. I had been thrust into a new world, one that didn't already have built into it all the protective walls I had always constructed around myself through the years.

One day, seeking a place of solitude far from the raucous student union, I drifted into the more comfortable Baptist Student Union. I'd been there for a "Howdy Party," and a couple of people I knew were always after me to get involved. I had been able to rebuff their cheerful advances, although one particular girl—Molly, from Wills Point, Texas—would not take no for an answer.

"Sorry," I always said. "That's just not me."

"You'd be surprised," she'd say. "You'd be real surprised what 'me' is when you let yourself relax and open yourself up to other Christians."

She meant well, I know, but the last thing I wanted to do was open up . . . to anyone. Too risky.

But silence *was* me, and it was sure quiet there that day, so I chose a spot in a far corner of the large common area, turned a chair to face away from the rest of the room and opened my book to study. And wouldn't you know it, an informal meeting began.

It began with prayer. Simple, short prayers about the needs of the students who were present. Financial needs. Ill parents. Difficult tests ahead. Career decisions to make. Then it became less practical and more personal. Loneliness. Depression. Fear. Then it broadened. Winning fellow students to Christ. Meeting the needs of international students. Being strong in the faith so "people can see Jesus in me." Amen.

Though not a part of the group, I listened, from my safe distance, to their discussion of the missionary journeys of the Apostle Paul, likening the events he was a part of to their daily walks across the huge campus.

"If our eyes are open, the needs are enormous," said the leader, a grandfatherly older man. "If our hearts are open, the provisions of God to meet those needs are even more enormous."

As the students left—to let others see Jesus in them—I sat quietly, hoping no one would see me, period.

"Hello there," he said, holding out his hand. "I'm Dr. Ware, associate director, and I'm glad you're here."

And I knew that he really was glad. For I could see Jesus in him.

I spent five years with Dr. Ware, taking every biblical course he taught as a professor, sitting through his Bible studies and devotional programs, traveling on mission trips and to student conferences, working on the leadership council with him. Somehow, he pulled me out of a shell so hard I had deemed it impenetrable, out of a hole so deep I had thought it bottomless. I learned to express myself. I learned to witness. I learned to love. I learned to say, with meaning, "I'm glad you're here," to lonely people who would drift into my life.

Dr. Ware comforted me during the tragedy of George's death. And, Dr. Ware stood before me with an open Bible and a rejoicing heart and joined me to my bride in the presence of the Lord we all served.

Dr. Ware . . . Dr. Russell Ware . . . was a guide. I named my second son for him, and I pray that he too will lead others to the King.

God used others to teach me of the goodness of men, slowly undoing the damage of my childhood.

Like Bill, a father-in-law who is the purest example I know of a godly man. Faithful to his wife, resistant to the whims of moral change, dedicated to his church and community, and full of love for his daughter. And her husband. And his grandchildren.

"He likes you," Lisa would say to me when her daddy would suggest I come riding with him in his truck to check on one of his gas stations or to fuel a plane at the airport.

One-on-one was still awkward for me, but he didn't care. Whether the conversation was the weather, the ball game, the impending arrival of another grandson, or the latest financial disaster Lisa and I were struggling with, it didn't matter. He was heavy on the listening, light on the advising, and very clear on one thing: "If you need me, I'm here."

Why? I thought. You're not my father.

No, he isn't. He is a Christian friend. And he is a guide.

There have been others. Like Merrill, a Christian banker who stuck beside me in a time of financial stress that almost destroyed my family. Along with financial assistance—both from the bank and from his own pocket—he offered observations and no-strings-attached advice.

"Why are you doing this for me?" I asked.

"Because I believe in you," he said.

Helping people borrow money was his occupation. But my debt to him was more than mere dollars. He was a guide.

I want to be a guide. I want to pray more. Learn more. Teach more. Give more. Reach more. But more than anything, I want people to see in my life a path that can help lead them to the King.

This starts in the home. I firmly believe the most damaging thing a man can do to the beliefs of his children is to practice something in public that he does not live in private. A man who prays on Sunday and is silent through the week; a man who encourages love on Sunday and doesn't practice it in the home or in the workplace or on the street; a man who gives on Sunday and takes all through the rest of the week; a man who smiles and hugs and pats his brothers on the back on Sunday, and then smirks and stabs them in the back all week; is a man who leads his children stumbling away from the path to eternal joy, dangerously close to another path, which also leads to eternity, an eternity of sorrow and remorse.

Thankfully, God uses other men to fill in the gap. Men like George, and Russell Ware, and Bill, and Merrill. The question is, Will there be enough if I am not one of them myself?

There is another man I want to mention. His name is Bob.

My mother married again, you see. A joyful Christian man, full of love for her and for the Lord, came into her life even as she grieved for George. God knew my mother could not be alone, so he sent her a man who would cherish her and love her.

She lives, because God loved her and provided for her, a more abundant life than ever. At a time when many people begin to feel their lives slowing down, she's speeding up. At a time when many people begin to dwell in the past, she's rewriting the future by taking advantage of every precious moment of the present. My mother has bloomed again, a brighter flower, a guide in her own right.

Sometimes life overflows with so much joy that "abundant" is an inadequate description. And sometimes life hurts so bad that there is no description. It is in these times that all of us need to know where God is. And sometimes, we just need someone to point the way.

Dear Lord, make me a guide. Help me get my act together. When it comes time for me to deliver my lines, let them help You lead the seeker to the King.

18
The Touch

"I want to eat the cracker and drink the juice," Patrick whispered to me as the deacon started down the aisle with the communion tray. "I want to take the Lord's Supper."

Patrick, who was eight, knew that the Lord's Supper was shared among Christians and was symbolic of their relationship with Him and their understanding that Christ had given up His life for them. I had told him before that someday he would rejoice in taking part in Communion, after he had asked Jesus to live in his heart and change his life.

The tray came closer.

"Don't worry, Dad," he said. "I am a Christian. I know Jesus. My heart's been changed."

And he took and he ate. And he took and he drank. My youngest son, my younger brother in Christ.

"My heart's been changed," Patrick had said. Was he repeating words he's heard in church since he was old enough to fill a spot in the nursery? How could someone with such a pure and innocent heart so full of goodness understand such change?

I believe it is harder for children who grow up in Christian homes to understand the changes wrought when people turn to Christ and surrender their heart and soul and seek a new will. It is not as if these children have turned from leading broken-down lives filled with sin to rise up again in newness of life. No, it is more an acceptance of the way it is supposed to be.

Patrick was new. His heart, he knew, had been changed. Yet by all outward appearances, Patrick was the same.

He was just a little boy, but Jesus had already healed him from hurts that would have come his way, diseases of the heart that would have robbed him of happiness, darkness that would have limited his vision, obstacles that would have stifled his walk. Patrick would have the privilege of reaching out to Jesus for all of his life.

As fathers or mothers, one of the most joyful moments of our lives is to see our children come to know the Lord. One by one, as they settle it, asking Jesus to live in their hearts eternally, our greatest responsibility is met. Accepted by us as miracles direct from God, our children are returned to Him to be fulfilled. To be changed.

"I don't feel so different," Patrick said. He knew he was, it just didn't show.

So I told him a story to help him understand this miraculous change that he knew had happened to him but couldn't really measure. It was the story of the long-suffering woman.

This poor woman could not remember a day before her suffering. For twelve years, she had bled. Nothing—no one, no physician—could ease her pain and humiliation. Twelve years. She asked herself: "Why can I not live like other women?" And she asked herself: "Why can I not die?"

It was as if she had never seen the sun. She had only felt its draining, blistering heat. She had only thirsted for life as the sun bore down upon her . . . but she had never seen it.

It was as if she had never noticed the flowers . . . only the weeds in her world's cracked, dry ground. She had never known the precious softness of the petals, the sweet perfume of the perfect bloom. No, her life was thorns and thistles . . . not blooms.

All she knew of life was that each day was worse than the one before.

And then . . . He came.

She was just one among the gathering crowd. She would never be noticed. But suddenly she knew with all her heart that if she could just move closer, just reach out and touch the hem of His garment, her suffering would end. The current of blood would cease to flow. Her fruitless search for a healing physician could end with that timid touch.

Faith flowed through her body as she fingered that fabric . . . and the bleeding stopped that instant. She thought her soul would burst with joy. But then, in the midst of that crushing crowd, He stopped, He turned, and she thought she would die.

"Who touched My clothes?" He asked gently.

She was horrified. She wanted to shrink, to disappear among the grains of hot sand on which she lay at His feet, trembling. She wanted never to have been . . . not to have had eyes to see that man . . . never to have had a heart to beat so uncontrollably in His presence.

"Who touched Me?" He asked again, so gently.

Then her eyes met His. Eyes so filled with love they overflowed into her own to see inside and wash away the years of painful sobbing. And she felt pure.

Despite her trembling, she told Him her story. That it was she who dared to touch Him. Despite the loudness of the crowd, He listened to every word.

"Your faith has made you whole," He said. "Go in peace and suffer no more."

Her faith. His touch.

Her heart, which beat uncontrollably out of fear only

a moment before, still beat uncontrollably, but out of joy now—the joy that flooded her soul as fear left her in the presence of Jesus.

And her soul? That tired shadow of a weary, regrettable life? In that touch . . . that soul became brand new. It crossed a burning desert to drink cool water from a well so deep it can't be measured.

Yes, she was new. Her eyes overflowed. Her heart pounded with a new power. Her soul rejoiced.

In an instant, twelve years of suffering became as nothing. It was over. Now she could see the sun. Now she could smell the sweet fragrance of the perfect flower. The dusty, dry sands of her life became the rich, moist soil of a new, fertile garden.

All because of that tender, timid touch. He was there . . . she reached out . . . and He turned to her.

Was she mortified? Yes, she was. Until she looked into His eyes. Until she heard His voice.

No longer mortified . . . she was glorified.

Because of the touch.

"You see, Patrick," I said. "Jesus touches people in exactly the way they need to be touched, because He knows all their pains and all their problems and all their needs.

"And even though it seems right now that you don't have a lot of pains, a lot of problems, or a lot of needs that your mom and I can't meet, Jesus knows about the ones to come. And when you reach out, like the woman did, He's gonna stop everything and turn to you. And, it's all because you believe in Him and know His name."

And then I told Patrick I loved him. That I loved being his daddy. That I loved him so much I would give up my life for him if I ever had to.

"Jesus already did," Patrick said quietly and with unusual dignity for an eight-year-old. And I knew that he knew. And my heart rejoiced.

19

On the Mountaintop

Somewhere in my youth—or childhood—I must have done something bad. Really bad. That's the only reason I could figure that I ended up in the back of the chartered bus, wedged against the bathroom, on a ten-hour church trip to the mountains of New Mexico.

What can I say? It had seemed like a good idea at the time. A week away from offices, responsibilities, freeways, red lights, television, telephones, barking dogs, Corn Pops, and growing grass. A week to hike, meditate, hear inspiring Bible teachers share God's Word, listen to beautiful music, sit quietly in the prayer garden under the aspens and the vast blue sky.

As I said, it seemed like a good idea at the time. But that time had not been envisioned as a 5:30 a.m. Saturday morning departure. That idea did not include sharing the back of the bus with an age group that averaged seven, none of whom had ever been on a bus with a potty. They were pretty excited about that and determined to give it a try. To help them in their determination, some wise and loving adult—sitting, no doubt up front right behind the driver—had placed a large cooler full of iced-down soft drinks.

"Help yourselves," he smilied to the adorables. "It's on me." Then he made his way back up the aisle. Bless his generous soul.

My role in life was reduced to freeing little ones from the potty when they realized it was much easier to get in than to get out. I also had the privilege of opening a million or two aluminum cans, chasing one down the aisle as it spewed forth its contents. That, of course, woke up some of the other adults, who looked at me as if I was the least considerate creature that had ever been inflicted on them.

It was interesting. Most of these people I had only seen on Sunday mornings. What a difference a day makes. I heard snores that could be taped for horror-movie sound effects. Another person, whom I had always pictured as kind of quiet, was on a personal mission to make sure no one slept, read, or put himself or herself through self-analysis.

And then there was Hugh, our devoted tour guide. Normally all suited up and semiserious as our church's director of education, he was the epitome of humor and patience. Even when Patrick reminded us all why you should never feed children Mexican food on long trips, Hugh just asked the driver to stop while the emergency was taken care of. He even moved his cooler so we could hose down the bus aisle.

"He *does* like children, doesn't he?" I whispered to Lisa as Hugh helped an embarrassed and freshly cleaned-up Patrick back on the bus.

"I think he likes people," she said. "And children are people."

Well, I was surrounded by people. Little ones, and though I had plenty, an awful lot of them weren't mine. I was shell-shocked. Every time I heard someone say "Dad?" I answered, no matter who said it.

By the time we got to Glorieta Baptist Conference Center, I was ready to skip all activities for the week and just pitch a tent in the prayer garden. By the end of that ride, I needed strength, courage, forgiveness, and plenty of time to repent.

We had made the decision to go to Glorieta last January, when it was cold and icy and there was not a green leaf or green blade of grass to be found. The skies had been gray for weeks. Just describe me as a model of depression. Glorieta, I was told, would replenish me. If I could hang on till summer.

I'd been there before, in college. I was single. So were all the nice, young coeds who went along to cook the meals and go for walks in the prayer garden. My Glorieta memories beckoned me to return.

"Do we have to go?" came the chorus from the children.

"Vacation?" said Zach. "You call that a vacation? That's like going to church every day."

"No TV?" said Russell, incredulously. "Where in the world is this place?"

"Are there bears?" asked Patrick. "If there's not any bears, I'm not going."

"Ten hours?" asked Donovan, leaning back against the wall and sliding to the floor. "And I bet we'll have to be like, super good the whole time. Is Brother Ted going?"

I told them about the time Lisa and I went, three months after we married, as sponsors for a student group from an all-women university.

"It was great," I said. "I was the only guy in this cabin full of college women. We had a great time."

Lisa was listening intently. I cleared my throat and sought a way to recover from my enthusiasm.

"Of course," I said, "the best thing was being married to your mom. That's really all I remember."

"Well, I don't see any reason for me to go," said Donovan. "I'm definitely not interested in falling in love."

The months passed and soon it was summer. The check for the expenses had cleared. We were going. Vacationwise, it was Glorieta or nothing. Second thoughts can't be taken to the bank.

Want to renew your appreciation for your own family? Take a long bus trip with everybody else's.

All good things come to an end, and so do bus rides. We arrived just as the coolness of the evening began to slide in over Mount Baldy. I could feel the responsibilities slipping away, the hurriedness of everyday life slowing down, the tension of the day-to-day dissolving. I could also feel every joint in my body unfolding as I tried to learn all over again how to walk after conforming to the alloted space between the cooler and the can.

Surrounded as we were by more space than any of us had seen in our lifetimes, it was a little deflating to find that our family of seven would lodge in one very nice, very average-sized room. We'd have two double beds and three roll-aways, and two inches between beds, just in case someone ever needed to get to the single bathroom.

"I like it," I said, trying to keep morale up. "And besides, it's close to the dining hall."

It was. Only about a city block uphill. Why, we could practically step out our door and get right in line. A long line.

That first night, after a great dinner, a spirit-rousing service, and an hour or so of laughter-punctuated unwinding conversation in the Chuckwagon, Day One ended.

The week sauntered by. It is amazing how much time there is in a day when it is not neatly divided up into work and play and eat and sleep and clean and cook and wash and fold and watch television and answer the phone and read the paper and run to the store and gas up the car and wash the kids and feed the dog and read a story and say good night and lock the doors and drift away. And start all over again.

That week, even with a schedule to follow, with all the necessary nuisances of life left behind in the lower altitudes, we discovered more about each other. There was time to walk together, talk together, play together, hike together, learn together, eat together, pray together, and very definitely, sleep together.

We were also there to learn to be better Bible-study teachers, and Lisa and I attended seminars during the mornings and afternoons while the children explored the hills and the valleys and the Scriptures with day-camp instructors. Zach, with the other teenagers, was absorbed in specially created activities designed to help young people strengthen their spiritual lives. Through the week of fellowship with other teens, he gained a clearer understanding of how vital his personal commitment to Christ would be if he and his energetic cohorts were to keep the Kingdom alive.

All week, Lisa and I went from conference to conference to conference, took the side trips with the other families to tour the Indian ruins, view the fish hatchery, cool our heels in the Pecos River, take in the laid-back Santa Fe market over an ice cream cone, eat the hottest Mexican food ever encountered in Albuquerque, hike up to Ghost Town, and end every evening at the Chuckwagon.

Finally, on the next-to-the-last day, we wound up in the prayer garden alone. We sat on a bench and watched the rabbits and the birds. Over near the waterfall, a young woman sat with her Bible open but her head bowed and her eyes closed. In the distance, just barely, we heard children laughing as they hiked the grounds and teenagers yelling on the volleyball courts.

Fifteen years had passed since Lisa and I made our first wedded trip to Glorieta. To the mountaintop. Joined by God forever. During those years, we'd visited an occasional valley filled with the stress of illness, the strain of financial uncertainty, the fear of change. And change we had, everything from establishing a new career to moving away from family to creating our own family, one by one by one by one by one.

"I don't know," I said to Lisa, "how nonChristians do it. I don't know how a man without a Christian wife can ever be happy. I don't know how children without Christian parents make it. I don't know how parents who don't have Christ within ever succeed."

For a little while, we didn't hear the laughing or the yelling. We didn't see the rabbits or the birds. It was a too-infrequent moment when we saw and heard each other and each other only. On the mountaintop.

When we came down from the garden, carrying pine-cone souvenirs, Lisa was crying softly. She should do that more often, I thought, knowing the tears were provoked by joy and peace. What we had come for. What we had found.

"What can I say?" I said. "This was a good idea."

We were on our way home, beginning a ten-hour descent. I was in the front seat of the bus, wedged between my bride and a window. And the world looked awfully good to me.

20
People of Capacity

A man I work with told me about the great care his daughter takes in choosing the Christmas tree for their home. It must have a beautiful scent; soft, moist needles; and an absolutely perfect shape. Every year, she is determined she will find the most beautiful tree they have ever had, surpassing the one from the year before.

His daughter has been blind since birth. She's never seen a Christmas tree, but is absolutely certain the one that adorns her living room is the most beautiful one in town. And according to her daddy, it is.

"Nobody," he says, his voice cracking under the weight of his love, "can choose a tree like my daughter."

I thought to myself, Wasn't God smart to put that daughter with that daddy?

Last year, there was a little girl in my sixth-grade Sunday school class who had to be carried up the stairs each Sunday morning that she was able to attend. Once there, she would smile and laugh and read her Bible and eagerly answer the questions asked. At prayer time, she would always list the needs of others and then, timidly, would add, "and please pray for me."

After class, her mother would be waiting at the bottom of the stairs with her daughter's wheelchair or crutches, whatever her condition called for at the time. It might be weeks before we would see her again, for she was frequently returning for more surgery.

Once, when I visited her in the hospital, she smiled and laughed and made jokes about the doctors and teased about the things her mother had said and done to get more attention for her daughter from the busy aides.

And I thought to myself, Wasn't God smart to put this mother with this daughter?

Not long ago, a couple I know buried their adult daughter. Struck with a very rare disease, she had lived with her parents for years, raising her own daughter. This beautiful woman suffered courageously until the disease finally ran its course and she went home to be with her Savior.

For years this family had spent evenings focusing on less painful times. She often told her mother she had had the happiest childhood any daughter could have dreamed of. Together they talked of the surety of Heaven and the love of God, and her father captured these moments in poetry to express his feelings and perpetuate her memory. On difficult days, her mother would distract her with funny stories while the nurses struggled with IVs and needles. This loving couple devoted their days to lessening the pain of this child they loved.

And I thought to myself, Wasn't God smart to put this couple with this daughter?

I know a little girl with a disease that makes it hard for her to grow, that robs her of her strength, that makes just breathing an exhausting chore. She is talented and sweet and has the spirit of an angel and the courage of a lion.

Day after day, her mother rubs her back to loosen her tired lungs, prepares her medicines, controls her environment, and makes sure she gets the rest she needs. Day after day, she makes sure her daughter gets the strength that can come only from love.

And I thought to myself, Wasn't God smart to put this mother with this daughter?

I know a man who suddenly lost his young wife in a tragic accident one morning just as a typical busy day was beginning. She had been a beautiful, loving, energetic woman, and they had agreed to spend their lives with each other, raising their four sons. Together, they had dedicated each son to the Lord. They had spent evenings dreaming of what God would do with each child, joyfully watching them grow and develop. Suddenly she was gone and he was on his own. Well, not entirely, for he knew he could draw on the strength of the Lord to teach him to carry on without his lifelong love at his side.

Gently he has helped his sons deal with their sorrow, carefully he has helped them rebuild their shattered lives, with wisdom he has guided them to reshape their routines, honestly and openly he is helping them deal with the permanent emptiness in their hearts so they will not be crippled by their loss. As he deals courageously with his own grief and loneliness, he is teaching them to be strong.

I remember the first day the father and his sons emerged from their private mourning. One of the sons had a ball game and they came to cheer him on, to support him, to restore some normalcy in the face of immense, immeasurable grief and loss.

I saw him again, a few months later, in a crowded department store with another of his sons, helping him choose a Christmas gift for someone special. A weary dad and his son, facing their first Christmas together without a wife and mother.

"I never knew," he said, shaking his head and smiling a mellow smile. "I just never knew everything she did."

But he's learning and he's determined and so full of love

for those boys that he will do everything God will empower him to do to make sure they grow up to be men who would honor their mother's dreams.

And I thought to myself, Wasn't God smart to put this father with these sons?

I know another couple whose dreams were rewritten only seconds after the birth of their first son. An accident? A complication? Questions crowded in, trying to replace their joy with doubt. But they were too strong. God had given them a son. God would help them deal with the challenges.

Friends stand amazed to see what this couple does on a daily, hourly basis to care for him, never knowing what they face in the future. His mother talks openly to God about her fear that she cannot handle anything more. But, she says, God always gives her sufficient strength to go on.

A year of tender, constant care later, they were sharing victories with their friends about how their son was responding. On Mother's Day they cried, because he smiled. They set no limitations for their son. God's power has no limits.

And I thought to myself, Wasn't God smart to put this couple with this son?

I imagine God looks over each child He sends into the world and considers carefully where he or she should go.

Perhaps the child needs a father with especially caring eyes to help her see what she cannot see on her own.

Perhaps the child needs a mother courageous and strong, so full of hope and faith that she can guide the child through pain and frustration and they can still both smile and laugh.

Perhaps the child needs a mother so patient and devoted that the demands created by her child's special needs become the clear, sharp focus of the mother's love.

Perhaps the child needs a father so sure in his faith in God that he can go beyond his own loss to provide an anchor when the steady ship of home is dashed about by tragedy.

Perhaps the child needs parents so grounded in God's love that they accept no earthly limits.

He looked at each of these children, and then He found the parents He knew could rise above despair, search for joy, and share it. He looked for people of capacity.

I am thankful that my children all can run and jump. They all can see and hear. I am thankful that only once I have had to sit in a hospital room and wonder why my child must bear such pain. I am thankful that I have not had to sit awake at night and listen to my child's painful breathing, wishing I could do it for him. I am thankful that I have never borne the grief of having a huge part of my life ripped away by the death of a loved one.

Maybe I have a capacity for quantity. That counts, too, I guess. I don't know the reasons why God looked down and decided to send these children to me, but I know He did. And in knowing that, I know that I must be what He wants me to be. They deserve the same depth of love, the same capacity for caring, the same devotion to meeting their needs, increasing their joy, soothing their despair, and comforting their sorrows as any child.

God so loves children that He has filled this world with people willing to shape their own lives to their children's needs.

People of capacity.

21
Play Ball!

Parents of Little Leaguers should automatically be given the right of way at all red lights and stop signs during the spring and summer. The very survival of modern civilization depends on getting to the fields on time—or at least before the starting lineup is set. Very few things in life are more important. Just ask Patrick, the screaming right fielder bouncing between the seat and the headliner in the back of the van.

Patrick's sitting next to his brothers, the center fielder and first baseman of two other teams. Only slightly more patient is our solitary soccer player, sitting next to me in the front. At least he knows he'll get to play from the very beginning because there are barely enough players on his team to take the field. So if he doesn't show up, he says, someone will likely come and burn our house down in the middle of the night. We take our sports seriously here in the land of the prevailing wind.

"A forfeit rests upon my shoulders," Donovan sighs. "All the dads are lined up on the sidelines, watching warmups, digging their toes in the dirt, putting their hands together, looking up at the sky and crying out, 'Where's Donovan?'

"It's kind of fun to save the day," he added. "No matter how I play, I always get at least one cheer—when our car pulls into the parking lot just before the ref can call the game off."

This is Oklahoma. These are kids. They gotta play. Something. Anything.

It was spring, and Zach, Russell, and Patrick signed up for baseball. All in different leagues, of course, just to make scheduling a sport in itself. Donovan stubbornly stuck to soccer. Lauren showed no interest in T-ball, settling instead for the sport of spectating. By summer's end, she'd earned a gold medal.

Don't get me wrong. I love the tastes, the sights, sounds, and smells of the ball fields as much as anyone. I've chewed a thousand pieces of baseball gum, sunburned my bald spot so many times it developed its own leather cover, plucked up a dozen sticky babies from the dirt under the bleachers— "Excuse me . . . is this one yours?"—and about pulled my arm out of the socket lugging coolers full of team drinks to practices. And once I sat in front of a lady who sounded like she was reciting a four-letter dictionary. Wow, the things she said in the name of team support!

And of course, sports participation is a year-round thing. Last fall, Zach played on the church-league junior-high basketball team. Every Saturday morning, much too close to sunrise, we slowly cruised through sleepy little neighborhoods on the far edge of the city.

"I don't know, Zach. I'm pretty sure I remember seeing that church around here somewhere. Isn't it the one with the pointy top and the gray trim?"

"Dad," he wailed. "The game starts in five minutes."

"I know what I'll do," I said brightly. "I'll stop and ask directions."

"Dad," he wailed again. "You've never been able to follow

directions. We're doomed."

Somehow, we found every church. We—he, rather—played every game. And soon it will be baseball season again. Nice.

Sportswise, it was a good year. Russell hit his first home run, and it sure was nice to hear someone other than me yelling, "Way to go, Russell!" I played in my first father-son baseball game, in which Zach pitched to me and I actually hit it. He made it impossible to miss. And throughout the season, Lauren and I, during slow innings, had the sweetest conversations on everything from the colors of butterfly wings to the relative slickness of suckers. Patrick gave me fresh insight into the meaning of sportsmanship when, after congratulating the other teams for "great games," he'd come over and ask me if his team had won. And every time Donovan, sporting his great individualism in his bright red-and-black checkered shirt, trotted out on to the soccer field, I felt a lump in my throat.

I am thankful for unselfish men and women who step in and prove to the sons and daughters of the athletically challenged that balls and bats were made for each other, that a person with a glove can actually pluck a speeding ball out of thin air, that a person can toss a round object at a high rate of speed across a field so close to another person that he can find that object without a map and compass.

A few years back, when Zachary was our only sports participant, I learned an important lesson in sportsmanship.

During the first few weeks of the season, Zachary's team stretched the talents and the patience of the coaches to the breaking point. There were a couple of boys on the team whose entire prior contact with the baseball had been to carry it from home to practice and back home again. But bit by bit, a team emerged.

I remember the first game in which Zachary's team heard the crack of the bat coming from someone who actually played on their team. Our dugout erupted. Leonard was so stunned he couldn't run. The coach almost wet his pants. The guys in their outfield woke up.

Weeks into the season though, there were no marks in the win column. But the margins were getting narrower. Parents cheered louder and louder. Pregame pep talks became more and more emotional. Then, it finally happened. The Mighty A's walked out in a cloud of dust and blew away the Tigers, 1-0.

They won five more games and got into a postseason tournament when another team dropped out. The playoffs. What a team.

Timothy was on that team. A fourth grader, like Zachary, he was one of the pitchers. A quiet, friendly boy. Well-liked. Just one of the guys.

Timothy and his dad were the first to arrive that fateful Friday night when the Mighty A's were to make their first-ever postseason appearance.

It was hot. The heat shimmered off the metal stands. The arid breeze stirred up the dirt on the pitcher's mound. Dusty trash swirled around the dugout fence. The snack bar's ice machine was broken. I'd rushed straight from the office, in a dark suit, without my sunglasses, only to find out there would be a one-hour delay. More good news: the coach had an emergency and couldn't make it.

From the looks of the boys, warming up out in the field, unaware of the unraveling going on, you would have thought it was a 70-degree spring day. They were throwing the ball from base to base, running after grounders in the outfield, swinging bats like they were cotton swabs. This was a team come to meet its destiny. Victory was written on their dirty faces in sweat . . . in cursive.

Nothing could destroy the confidence they had in each other. As a ball plopped into a glove, there was always a shout of "Way to go!" or "Awesome catch!" As they rounded the bases, just warming up, they tapped each other on the shoulder and told each other over and over again, "We'll get 'em this time." This was Zach's team, boys every bit as cocky as he.

Timothy's dad, Robert, stepped foward and came to the rescue.

"I'll coach," he said. "No problem."

Before the hour was up and the game time came, Robert had shifted the lineup, moved some of the starters to the bench and taken Timothy from the end of the pitching rotation and made him the starter.

Parents were up in arms. Players were down in the dumps. Team spirit was on a slow boat to China.

One brave parent came forward and told Robert he was damaging the team, that things should have been left just as the coach had done it all season.

"All season," said Robert. "The way the coach did it all season is why we have a record of six wins and ten losses. I tried to tell Lambert how to run this team and he wouldn't listen. Well, he's not here today and I'm the coach."

Suddenly, the record the boys had been so proud of—those six hard-fought wins—looked like nothing. The team sank deeper on the hot metal benches. The boys looked very small.

Two more parents came forward and suggested maybe Robert was not the best choice for fill-in coach. Perhaps he should be third-base coach . . . or maybe even find a comfortable seat in the sticker patch beyond the outfield fence. It was getting hotter.

"All right," Robert said. "I won't coach. And," he said with a victorious smirk, "Timothy won't play. Come on, son, let's watch these guys lose. Then we can go home."

Timothy stood alone by home plate, his head hanging low as his glove dropped off his hand and thudded into the dirt. His teammates looked from parent to parent with stunned expressions of disbelief that said "Can he do that? Can he take Timothy out of the game just because he can't coach?"

He could. And he did. And they lost the game. Not because Robert didn't coach. And not because Timothy didn't play. They lost because no one really played. They couldn't catch, throw, run, bat, or pitch. They were hot, thirsty, and tired. They were extremely irritable and discourteous to the other team. And then the season was over and the miserable parents took their miserable boys home.

On that hot Friday evening I learned a difficult truth. I learned that there are some parents who just have no intention of really listening to their children. Not like some of us, who accidentally pay too little attention sometimes, or hear something different from what was really said because we're temporarily distracted with some problem of our own. No, these parents make a regular practice of not listening. Often, they are the same parents who make such a show of their concern, parading themselves as champions of child-rearing. They haven't a clue.

Timothy had never said a word. But when his shoulders slumped and his head fell forward and his glove plopped into the dust, he was screaming for help with all his being. Sometimes kids are stuck with parents who just can't hear.

Timothy had such a parent.

22
Head of the House

Patrick doesn't take too many things seriously, but occasionally something grabs hold of him and he just won't let it go. He will question an idea or concept until he is satisfied that society isn't misleading him and that all is right in his world.

I'm never prepared for his persistence.

"Dad, can we go to the movies today?" he asked as we crawled slowly down a very optimistically named Northwest Expressway.

"Maybe," I said. "I'll check with Mom when we get home."

"She'll say no," he said. "She'll say we need to clean our rooms, or read a book, or play outside in the sun. Or . . . or something else."

The tires on the van made a couple of rotations as we progressed toward home.

"Dad?" asked Patrick. "Can we get another hamster?"

What a radical idea. We hadn't had a hamster die on us in weeks.

"Well, maybe," I answered. "We'll see what Mom thinks."

I turned off the radio.

"Dad?" came the voice again. "Can we eat out tonight?"

"Probably," I said. "If Mom doesn't already have something planned."

I pushed a cassette tape into the player.

"Dad?" Patrick asked again. "Is Mom the head of our house?"

Wham! I felt like I was in a ten-car pileup. My face was turning red. My temperature was rising. I was suddenly feeling very closed in by the cars surrounding me. I looked in the rear-view mirror. Patrick was perched in the middle of the seat behind me, an innocent little grin on his face.

"Patrick," I said, "I am the head of the household. I make the decisions. And don't you forget it. Understand?"

"Okay," he said. "Does that mean we can eat out, go to the movies, and pick up a new hamster on the way home?"

He'd set me up. And I almost fell for it. He was watering down the parent partnership, looking for a crack in which to stick a wedge, testing a biblical concept, and for convenience' sake, looking for a little personal gain in the process.

What do pizza, hamsters, and big-screen fantasy have to do with whether or not I am fulfilling my role as the head of the family? I asked myself that question as I zeroed in on the bumper in front of me. I slammed on the brakes and avoided the accident. Fortunately, we were at the expressway's top speed of seven miles an hour.

For scoring purposes, we did eat out that night and we did go to a movie. But we decided to put the used hamster cage in a garage sale and declare "no more fur." "We" made those decisions, his mother and I.

This "head of the household" thing is very touchy to me. When I was growing up, there was never any doubt. Mother was the head of the household. But there was another thing that was never in doubt, and that was that she had never intended it to be that way. It was not her natural role. She was supposed to have had a partner. She understood the concept of the helpmeet. And she would have made a wonderful complement to a committed head of the household.

"You must be a man," she would tell me when I was a teenager. "Take the responsibility, don't run from the decisions, love your wife, cherish your children."

And be the head of the household.

So I always wanted to be the head of the household, ruler over all I surveyed, supreme commander, father and master over my many loyal subjects. I carried this dream to the altar and later into the delivery room . . . five times. My kingdom went from squalling to crawling to sprawling all around me.

So, if I am the head of the household, why is the head aching and the house barely holding together? And if I am the head of the household, why do I sometimes go to bed with dishpan hands and worry that I've forgotten to unplug the iron?

If I am the head of the household, why do I have to barter for time to watch a football game on television, promising to ride bikes for two hours in exchange for ten minutes of solitude?

And, if I am the head of the household, why do I have to cut my subjects' plates of meat after I set the table? And why do I have to clear the table and pick up mushy mashed potatoes from the floor with my bare hands while everyone else has dessert they weren't supposed to get unless they ate all their mashed potatoes?

And, if I am the head of the household, why do I have to wash sand out of the bathtub every morning before I can shower? And why is there no soap on my rope? And why does someone keep using my toothbrush to scrub the wheels on his roller blades?

And, if I really am the head of the household, why am I always seventh in line for the bathroom when it's in working order, but first in line when Lauren plays washing machine in the potty, sending our best towels to septic heaven?

And, if I really am the head of the household, why am I

always buckling bodies into the van and heading down the highway to places I don't really want to go to spend money I really don't have on things I really don't want to buy?

And if I'm really his majesty, why must we eat at McDonalds?

And if I'm really top dog in this daddy's domain, why do I rush around during commercials switching clothes from the washer to the dryer; feeding the dogs; tracking down the hamster; folding underwear, slips, etc.; fetching glasses of water up the stairs; and tripping over the well-placed traps on the stairway?

And, if I am the head of this house, why do I have to cover five other bodies before I pull my own blanket up to my own chin; explain away everybody else's nightmares before I take on my own; fluff their pillows and tuck their feet back under the sheets; get them one more drink; and plug in their nightlights?

And if I am the head of the household, why do I have to rub her back before she can go to sleep?

Why, I ask? Why do I have to do all these things? Because I am the head of the household, that's why.

Patrick wonders why I don't just issue proclamations, make off-the-top-of-my-head decisions and rule with the iron fist afforded my position. Because my responsibility, as head of the household, is to demonstrate my love, show my faith, proclaim my hopes, share my prayers, and strengthen my family. And I can't do that with an iron fist. I must do it with a willing heart, open ears, outstretched arms, and kind, caring eyes to see the needs and dreams of the people God put in my household.

If I don't listen . . . if I am inconsiderate of others . . . if I make decisions without the input of the wife God gave me . . . if I try to do it on my own without God, then I may as well forget about being the head of the household.

That's what I'll tell Patrick next trip down Northwest Expressway. We'll have plenty of time.

23

Living on the Edge

I've searched my memory banks, more than once, and cannot find a single record of anyone ever telling me that being a parent would be easy. Rewarding, yes. Enjoyable, yes. Enlightening, yes. Challenging, for sure. Easy? No way.

It's a good thing nobody ever told me that because, this being the litigation era, I would have a pretty good case. Anyone who has had children for more than a day knows parenting is about as easy as swimming the backstroke across the Atlantic Ocean.

No one ever bothered to warn me that there would be occasions when I really wouldn't like some of these people very much. Not that there aren't plenty of occasions when the feeling is mutual. All of us, in our own turn and in our own way, can be quite unlikable. Thank God—literally—that love is sufficient to carry us through the deepest depths of familial tribulation.

The other morning, Donovan was pounding keys on the piano and "singing" at the top of his untrained lungs. I cut him off with one of my headache looks.

"I'm the Donnie, gotta love me," he said.

"You've been watching too much television," I growled. "Go read a book."

But he's right. He *is* the Donnie. And I *gotta* love him. Just like I gotta love the Zach and the Russell and the Patrick and the Lauren. And the Mommy, who, also on occasion, tests the limits of oneness. Like that same morning.

"You guys really need to be kinda quiet this morning," I whispered to the boys at breakfast. "I think your mother's a little on edge. We passed in the hall a minute ago and I'm not sure she recognized me."

"Dad?" asked Donovan. "What's it mean to be on edge?"

"I think it means Dad's in trouble," said Russell. "Or, it means Mom's having one of her mean days."

"Shhh," Zachary hissed. "Here she comes."

"GET YOUR FINGERS OUT OF THE BUTTER," Lisa said with *feeling*, sending Lauren into trembles. Lauren's body went nearly limp and her whole hand, as a fist, sank deep into the Bluebonnet margarine tub.

"That settles it. I'm not eatin'," said Zach, looking at Lauren's buttered hand.

"You like living?" giggled Russell, glancing sideways at his mother. "You better eat."

"Don't laugh at the table," said Lisa.

A new rule?

Patrick arrived at the table with a hamster in his hand (yes, another hamster).

"Return that animal to the cage," Lisa commanded, sending shivers down little Snuggles' furry spine. "And wash your hands before you come back to the table."

Not nearly soon enough, breakfast ended and the boys disappeared in a flash, leaving Lauren licking her buttery fingers, Lisa glaring, and me hoping for another day on this good earth.

By the time the dishes were done, Lisa settled down,

having satisfied her edge by sifting through the kids' toys to find some things to throw away. I could tell it was making her feel better.

About 9:00 a.m.—it seemed like noon at least—Donovan came screaming through the front door holding his head in his hands.

"Zachary hit me," he wailed. "He tried to kill me!"

"What did you do to him?" I asked.

"Nothing," he sobbed. "I just borrowed his roller blades and crashed into the van. I thought he was coming to help me get up, but he hit me instead."

"Well," I said, trying to be comforting. "I think maybe Zachary's just a little on edge about something."

About that time, I heard Patrick shrieking from the garage. While I determined his life was not in danger, there was a real edge of despair in the air, so I hurried out, whereupon I found Russell sitting on top of him with a paintbrush.

"Get off of him!" I shouted at Russell, trying to hide the fact I was mostly worried about paint getting smeared all over the garage floor. No doubt Patrick deserved a good touch-up job.

"No," replied Russell calmly. "I've decided I really am going to paint him. He deserves it. He called me a boogernose and threw a rubber ball at my bicycle spokes when I was turning into the driveway. He tried to kill me."

Russell's paintbrush was perilously close to Patrick's nose. I remembered how Patrick's day had started, with his mother launching into him for inviting Snuggles to breakfast. He was really having a bad day.

"Now Russell," I said, trying to calm him. "You're just a little on edge. You really don't want to paint Patrick sierra brown. We'd have to leave him out in the yard because he'd match the house trim."

"Oh yes I do," said Russell. "I'm going to paint him."

Being "on edge" is among Russell's natural talents. I

grabbed the brush, whereupon Patrick squirmed away just as Russell lunged for the can of WD-40.

"If I catch you, Patrick, we'll never hear another squeak out of you," Russell yelled, can in hand.

Thirty minutes later, as Donovan and I were sitting in the living room—I was trying to explain to him what "on edge" means—we heard a thundering thud and a piercing shriek.

"Dad," Donovan whispered. "Look. Mom's on the floor."

And, by gosh and by golly, she was. She had fallen down the last couple of steps and was sitting in a whimpering pile at the bottom of the steps, massaging her left foot and nearing a meltdown.

"She looks kinda dangerous to me," I said to Donovan. "Approach with caution."

Donovan laughed.

It was not the right moment for laughter.

When I realized Lisa really had hurt herself, I offered comfort. It must have had a hollow ring to it. She hopped up and hobbled away, leaving us all staring after her.

Rebuffed, I went on about my business, trying to convince Russell to put away the WD-40 so Patrick could come back down from the tree.

Since all was going so well at home, I went to the office for a while. You know, to catch up on some urgent things that just couldn't wait.

I was gone about two hours when the phone rang.

"It's broken," Lisa whimpered.

"What's broken?" I asked, picturing my twenty-year-old, unopened souvenir Dallas Cowboys Super Bowl Dr Pepper bottle shattered on the floor.

"My toe," she said, her voice cracking. "I went to the doctor and had it x-rayed. It's broken."

Lisa doesn't often get hurt. Parents aren't supposed to do that. It's just too inconvenient. That must be why when she hobbled off to the bedroom, I just assumed her ego had sustained the greatest damage. After all, parents aren't supposed to stumble on the stairs either.

Suddenly, I felt terribly guilty.

"Put your foot up and I'll be right home," I said. "Don't worry about cooking supper. I'll cook. And don't iron. I'll do it. You just sit back and relax."

I hurried home, just as I had promised. Lisa's misfortune had done little to calm the homefront. Russell and Donovan both had science projects due Monday. They were feeling the strain, arguing over the use of everything from the computer to the colored markers. Zach was dressed and ready for basketball practice, pointing unsympathetically to his watch. Lauren had a cough and a temperature. Snuggles had disappeared and Patrick was already well into the mourning phase.

Lisa needed a pain prescription filled. A computerized recording kept calling me up to sell life insurance. Nobody had turned on the dishwasher. All the food was frozen.

"I don't think you really care about my toe," she said.

"Why couldn't I have broken my toe?" I exclaimed with all the sympathy left in me. "Why can't I sit on the couch and just watch a whole generation unravel in front of me? Why . . . why . . . why?"

As I put on my coat, searched the house until I found the keys to go get some pizza, Mary, Lisa's friend and sympathizer, arrived at the door with a homemade spaghetti supper—even fresh French bread. I have often heard of the importance women place in having close friends. That night, I was all for it.

"Hi, Donnie," Mary said as she carried the food to the kitchen. "What's wrong with your daddy? He looks upset."

A light went off in Donnie's little head.

"I think he's on edge," he said. "Yes, I believe he's on edge."

24

Nothing More Beautiful

I n the dark of night, I awoke. Framed in the moonlit, lace-curtained window, I saw my child and his mother, sharing a rocker at midnight, only the moon and I to spy. My intrusion was silent, but it fulfilled my need for joy.

She kissed her baby's fingers first, then opened the tiny hands and kissed the palms. Then she took her own graceful fingers and traced gently across the tiny eyelids, down the soft cheeks, and around the bottom of the dimpled chin. She gently kissed his nose, smoothed his hair, and then just held him to her, an external closeness that reminded them both of the nine months they spent together alone.

They looked into each other's eyes and smiled. His tiny hands reached out for her face. I smiled too, and slept.

Later, the soft cry of my son awakened me. Soon, he once again succumbed to the soothing rituals of his mother, all his needs met.

I was almost asleep again when I heard more sniffling. I quietly watched my wife, in kinship with her newborn son, cry her own soft tears, a physical expression of inner peace and joy. My own eyes filled as I secretly shared the scene.

And suddenly I knew: A mother's tears are never wasted. They express joy and happiness, soothe, mend, break down barriers, share pain. A mother's tears relieve frustration so the work of mothering can go on . . . and on . . . and on.

It's the legacy of countless generations of ladies in rocking chairs, bathed in moonlight.

It's the fulfilling truth of a mother's midnight tears of joy, wiped from her gentle eyes with the corners of soft blankets, pink and blue.

It's the unbreakable promise of permanent, powerful love, sealed with the first soft kiss on a tiny nose at midnight.

Those joyful tears and that silent promise create a bond more powerful than anything beyond that moonlit window. An awesome strength to last a lifetime springs forth from such a soft beginning.

In all the world, I believe there is nothing more beautiful to see than a sleeping child. Except to see his mother, as she watches.

❖

In the bright midday sun, I sat inside my room. Framed in the sunshine, outside the window, I saw my child and her mother, sharing a muddy garden, only the flowers and I to spy. My intrusion was unnoticed, but it fulfilled my need for joy.

She pulled her daughter's tangled hair back and tied a ribbon in it, slowly fingering her bangs. She touched each cheek and then her chin and pecked her on the nose with a gentle kiss. They paused and looked at each other and then collapsed against each other in giggles. A private, perfect moment.

On hands and knees, they sorted through the flowers and plucked the weeds from the soil, seeking to create beauty. And then, spurred on by Lauren's fascination, they began to dig for worms.

Her mother picked a flower and placed it in her daughter's hair. Lauren picked a flower and repaid the favor. More giggling.

Soon they set aside the hoes and trowels and replaced them with tales and memories. I couldn't hear, which is as it should be, for they were sharing with each other and I was but a silent benefactor.

In all the world, I believe there is nothing more beautiful to see than a laughing child. Except to see her mother, as she watches.

❖

In the dusk of the day, I came quietly through the door. Framed in the light of the fireplace, I saw my children and their mother, sharing a snack and a story as the day wound down to night. My intrusion was unnoticed, but it fulfilled my need for joy.

With her hands she gestured to embellish the points of her story. With gentle eyes she looked from child to child, bringing them all in to share the warmth of the fire and the tale of her own younger days.

Enthusiasm built as she passed out marshmallows and they began to roast them over the logs, listening as she told of doing the same when she was a little girl.

In all the world, I believe there is nothing more beautiful to see than a curious, wondering child. Except to see his mother, as she watches.

❖

In the dark of night, I awoke. Framed in the moonlit, brightly curtained window, I saw my child and his mother, sharing a frightening dream at midnight. My intrusion was silent, but it fulfilled my need for joy.

Where once she had kissed his baby fingers, she now rubbed his strong shoulders. Where once she had traced her graceful fingers across his tiny eyelids, she now looked deeply into strong, forceful eyes. Where once she had gently kissed his nose, she now pushed back his hair from his face and kissed him gently on the forehead.

The muffled call of her son had awakened her, just as it had fourteen years before. And, just like fourteen years before, he succumbed to the soothing voice of his mother, all his needs met. Someone to come in the darkness, listen, adjust the covers, pray for angels' protection and good dreams, and disappear back down the stairs. He does not often awaken in the night and had almost forgotten the fulfillment of being treated like a child. With only the two to witness, he can accept her comfort.

Tomorrow he may forget what he dreamed, but he will never forget that she listened.

From my own bed, I listened as my wife, alone in the night, walked through her house, straightening covers and pillows, turning on nightlights, adjusting heaters, tightening windows, picking up toys left in thoughtless places, ending the drip of a faucet. The soft padding of her house shoes comforts me as they make their way toward our room.

It's the legacy of countless generations of ladies, pulling the covers tight around their homes, padding softly in the moonlight.

It's the fulfilling truth of a mother's midnight sighs, marked with satisfied, gentle eyes.

It's the unbreakable promise of permanent, powerful love, whether it be sealed with the first soft kiss on a newborn's tiny nose or on the hard, strong forehead of a comforted teenager.

In all the world, I believe there is nothing more beautiful than a mother, as she loves.

25

Don't You Dears Know What Causes This?

Sons are a heritage from the LORD,
children a reward from him.
Psalm 127:3, NIV

W e stopped to eat on our way home from Texas where we'd gone to wear out our relatives. I hopped out of the car and headed into the restaurant with three sons—seven, five, and four. We were so cute.

Behind us, lagging a little, struggled a very pregnant Lisa with our fourth son, a two-year-old, in tow. They were so cute.

I had the urge to sit at a separate table from my wife, just to escape the stares and the questions from the curious.

"Are they all yours?"

"Still trying to get that girl?"

"Don't you dears know what causes this?"

"Yes, no, yes."

The night before, we'd gone to Dallas to take the kids to a huge, new shopping mall. Russell wanted to ride the escalator, which rose two stories above the ice skating rink. As we ascended, we noticed people politely pointing at us and smiling. We were so cute.

But family life is not always cute. Sometimes it turns

sad, or depressing, or confusing, or painful. Other times though, it just turns over and spills out joy. Sometimes love just stops us right in our tracks and overwhelms us.

Did we plan to have five children? No, we didn't. Did we really keep trying till we got our girl? No, we didn't. In fact, she was to be Cameron. We were so certain that our fifth son was on his way that we didn't seriously consider girls' names at all.

That's what happens when we get caught up in our own certainty. God has His way with us, just to make our lives a little more abundant.

By the time Lauren arrived, I was an old hand at birthing babies. In the presence of God and a doctor, I had already cut four umbilical cords, accepting four beautiful baby boys as ours.

But when Lauren came, I almost dropped the scissors. I forgot everything I had learned in four birthing procedures. I didn't want to cut the cord. What if it hurt her? She was too beautiful. She was not Cameron. She was my daughter. She was downright scary.

That was six years ago. During those six years, I have had to just sit down every now and then and scratch my head in wonder.

"She must be awfully tough with all those brothers to put up with," people say.

No, I think. She has such a tender heart.

"She must be awfully protected with all those brothers watching after her," people say.

No, I think. She's awfully tough.

Tough and tender. My girl.

Another not-so-still small voice.

My family is complete now. It feels that way. The doors open and my children come from all directions to a crowded table or to track down their laundry or to crowd into the van. My children.

"Are they all yours?"

"You bet. And God bless them, every one."

On a cold winter Sunday afternoon, I took my oldest son, now fifteen, out into the front yard. We were sharing a football.

"I can kick it higher than you," he said. "Farther than you. Straighter than you."

And he tried. And he kicked it higher than the utility pole and halfway down the street. He retrieved the ball, and with a satisfied grin, handed it to me and said, "Here, Dad, top that."

"Watch this," I said, laughing at him. And I kicked the ball over our house. Our two-story house.

And I retrieved the ball, and with a satisfied grin, handed it to him and said, "Here, Zach, top that."

And he did. He kicked it higher and he kicked it farther . . . over the two-story house and far into the back yard.

And then we went into the warm house . . . together.

Author

Thom Hunter is a journalist, having been on both sides of the fence, first as a newspaper reporter and now as a spokesman for Southwestern Bell Telephone. Still, he says, despite twenty years of working professionally with words, the antics of his five kids sometimes leave him speechless.

The product of a childhood he describes as "the definition of difficult," Thom's goal as a writer is to help parents experience the joy and develop the promise of each child. *Those Not-So-Still Small Voices* is Thom's second book. His first was *Like Father, Like Sons, and Daughter, too*, published by Revell.

Thom majored in journalism and English at North Texas State University in Denton. He is a deacon at Village Baptist Church in Oklahoma City, where he has taught sixth grade Sunday school for five years.

Thom and his wife, Lisa, live in Oklahoma City with Zachary, Russell, Donovan, Patrick and Lauren, a couple of tree crabs, a turtle, a lizard, a hamster, some cats, and who knows what else.